BULK ORDERS

Requesting a Bulk Orders of this book is easy:

Simply visit our website at:

www.wells2000llc.com\bulk

We offer discounts on orders of 50 copies or more.

Depending on current volume we will respond within 1 Business Day from receipt of your request.
(Response time may increase or decrease depending on the size of the request.)

Please note: Bulk orders are non-returnable.

a SURVIVOR'S FIELD GUIDE *to* MILITARY SEXUAL TRAUMA

A Survivor's Field Guide to Military Sexual Trauma

www.wells2000.com
www.JustCrafty.com

Because of the dynamic nature of the Internet, any Web addresses or links contained in this book may have changed since publication and may no longer be valid.

ISBN-10: 0983706549
ISBN-13: 978-0-9837065-4-0

I praise God, and my Lord and Savior Jesus Christ, for constantly being there for me.

I thank my husband, Doug, and children, Treg and Shante', for being my fortitude.

In Memory of my Battle Buddy, no matter the peril we encountered – my Military Working Dog, "Killer, I will always adore and remember you."

I need to acknowledge Zorro, another Military Working Dog, for attacking his handler when the perp sexually assaulted me. "Thank you Zorro, you deserved better."

To all my brothers and sisters-in-arms, past and present, who have experienced MST, you are always in my prayers.

CONTENTS

1

ME

A brief bit about me. I am not a keyboard warrior. I enlisted in the Air Force right out of high school, but the AF put me on the delayed enrollment program for 6 months until I turned 18. Like all other Airman, I went to Basic Training at Lackland AFB, Texas. I also completed my Law Enforcement and Military Working Dog Handler technical school, there as well. I spent a month in Ft. Dix, New Jersey for Air Base Ground Defense, trained by the Army.

Then off to my first and only permanent duty station, Dyess AFB, Texas. There I was assigned my (MWD), Killer B-478. I was at Dyess only a few months and sent for 3 months on a TDY to Howard AFB, Panama. Exactly one year later, I was again sent on another 3 month TDY to Panama, but this time Operation Just Cause was going on. A few months back at Dyess and off again on another TDY to Saudi Arabia, Jeddah, for Operation Desert Shield/Storm.

I was the only female handler at Dyess, the entire time that I was there. When I went to Panama the first time, I went with two other handlers from Dyess. My second TDY to Panama I went alone. The TDY to Saudi was with three handlers from my base. In Saudi I was not only the only female hander, but a week after I arrived I was the only female Security Police officer in my entire squadron, and it stayed that way for three months when another female SP (Security Specialist) arrived. I only saw her once, and never asked about any other female SPs, but since her unit was the only additional one who came just prior to Operation Desert Storm in January, I believe she was it.

I was sexually harassed right as I set foot into Basic Training. I was then sexually assaulted in Basic Training. And from the first day I was in Law Enforcement training, I was sexually discriminated against. My entire enlistment was riddled with sexual discrimination, sexual harassment and sexual assaults. I swear that they were all part of my career field, since no matter where I went, or what branch I was working with, it continually was present.

From outside my squadron, I was awarded Outstanding, Excellence, Letters of Appreciation, Certificates of Appreciation, medals, ribbons, and more. I completed my CDCs, EOC, QC, and fifth level with outstanding and excellence in marks. I qualified expert on all weapons put in my hands. My MWD, Killer, who was a dog fighter, massive, man-hating ball of fury, loved and obeyed me, which most detested even more. The more I did, the better I was shown to be, the worse it got.

I was discharged with a 39-10 (Pattern of Minor Disciplinary Infractions) General, Under Honorable Conditions Discharge. A type of discharge you get when you really didn't do anything wrong, but the command does not like you, for one reason or another. The Article 15 I received was for not cleaning or watering my dog's kennel, on some day, around the time, before I was hospitalized in Saudi Arabia. It was the complete idea of a setup, try and fight when there is no time listed, no date listed, and normally only K-9 Handlers go into the kennels. Which made it understandable when the handlers, who wrote the statements against me, were the ones pushing for the Article 15. Since they were the ones I put in the reports for the assault, the harassment and the discrimination.

I did not keep quiet when regulations were disregarded. I did not keep quiet when I was sexually discriminated against (at Dyess). I did not keep quiet about the corruption of my unit at Dyess. I was not quiet about the corruption in Panama. I was not quiet about how sexual assault reports were handled. I was not quiet when I was sexually assaulted, sexual harassed and sexually discriminated against in Saudi. I did my job, was very good at it, and kept my military bearing and standards above the others. But was discharged all the same.

I now have service-connection for some of the disabilities, which I suffer from, that occurred during my military time. I am not the person who went into the military, or into Basic, or tech school, or even that went to Saudi. I have been profoundly changed by those experiences. I have been an advocate for women veterans and MST survivors since 1991. I have privately written since 1991 about how the military treats victims, and since 1998 publically. I have written: *Crossing the Blue Code*; *Beyond the Blue Code*; *MST* (2009); *MST Revised* (2011); *Military Sexual Trauma* (2012); *Understanding Military Sexual Trauma* (2013); this book, and will have my next one *A Survivor's Workbook to Military Sexual Trauma*, by the end of this year (2016) or hopefully the first of next year. I am trying. Which them and more can be viewed and purchased through my main website – JustCrafty.com. All proceeded from any of the purchases from my businesses go directly to helping veteran women and MST survivors. I pretty much stay in the background, and I do like it like that. I have good and bad days, but I hope in what I have learned, I can help others, to share what I know with all in need.

The Lord uses a scale very different from the world's to weigh the worth of a soul. - Dieter F. Uchtdorf.

Confidentiality

I am very serious about the confidentiality of all the people who tell me their stories. I do not use anyone's information, unless they have given permission. When I am participating in therapy (in groups), the information will not be in these books. There are so many stories which are so similar, and have events seemly with the same details, but I will never divulge what has been communicated in private.

When I am in groups, I am there for my own personal healing. So, I ask the same from all. If you are hearing another's story, know that you have been privileged with a special trust, and keep it as you would your own. With that said, there are many of us who are mandated by law to notify the proper authorities, if we hear specific abuses, which are ongoing. I would plead that if any of you hear these abuses to not keep quiet, it is just as wrong as the abuse itself. Help out those who are suffering, help the innocent and treat all with the divine worth, we all possess.

Honor is doing the right thing,
knowing that nobody is going to know if
you did it or not. -Me

2

GETTING STARTED

This book is not a substitution for psychotherapy, it is intended to be an added help on your therapeutic journey. I love all my VetSisters and all my Sisters-in-arms, (believe me when I do say that I do deeply love you all) and want only the best for all of you. I understand not everyone will have the same opinions or recommendations that I put forward; however, after considerable time praying, I am strong in my conviction that this book will help you. Please know it is done out of love and concern, if offense is taken, it is not intended, but I would not be true to who I am if I restricted myself into presenting politically correct information. And you would not get the valuable advice needed. I do not hold back the reality and because of that, my name has been used for good and evil. I am fine with that. I am who I am, and I am eternally jubilant of that.

I am not what happened to me... I am what I choose to become. – C.G. Jung

---

I was doing my normal highlighting and note taking in the margins, in some book and the person watching me gasped. She said she always made sure her books were as new looking when she was done as when she purchased them. When I further questioned it sprang from her childhood at school, the books had to be treated with the greatest of respect and returned as they were given. I asked if it helped if someone gave her permission to do what she wanted and she laughed but after a while said it would. So, I give permission to you to use this book in the manner that is best for your healing journey. Librarians would be mortified looking through my books –

writing, highlighting, doodles, dog ears, folded pages and even the mishap of what I happened to be drinking at the time. I transform these cleanly printed pages into something more than what they were, to be uniquely mine. I give you permission to do the same.

All English majors, or people who accept and use the complexities of grammar correctly, need to realize that English is my second language. I do not know what my first language was, but ask all my English teachers and they will attest it was not English. I am a math person, I know it. English is a foreign language, and so if you are a stickler for grammar, I ask that you turn off that switch while reading this. This book is written like I speak, and think. It is purposeful. I want you to have the feeling that I am with you, speaking face to face, and hearing my thoughts, as we go through this journey together.

When you have been given something helpful, you normally are told to put it into your toolkit. I have never liked that metaphor. To me when someone says get the toolbox, it is to fix or build something. On a journey, this journey, you will need to figure out where it is you want to go, then make a map for getting there. Sometimes all you can put down is the final destination as a vague statement. You have not yet determined the details, the small towns you'll go through. You cannot see the detours or the road work that is out there. Some of the road signs are there allowing time to slow down, other times you go over a hill and there is a wreck on the other side that necessitates immediate attention. This map gets put where? A toolbox? No. I like a backpack better. Inside your backpack, on this journey, you have the toolbox, but much more resources than you may need. There is substance, food, water, protective weather gear, but all is inside what you carry with you. That is why I like the backpack instead of the toolbox. So, pick up your backpack and get ready to put in your resources and let's had off on this journey together.

Have not I commanded thee? Be strong and of a good courage; be not afraid, neither be thou dismayed: for the Lord thy God is with thee whithersoever thou goest. – Joshua 1:9

Safety First!

I start out with safety because your safety during your journey should always come first. In order to progress on this journey it is fundamental to establish a framework of emotional and physical safety. The essential core foundation to help you progress into your new self is built on safety. Safety is something you must consider on a daily basis; in your home, at work, with your family, and even alone with yourself.

The path you are taking to become your divine potential, involves facing dreadful memories, horrible painful feelings, at times what can seem like overwhelming bodily sensations, and the possibility of self-destructive compulsions and behaviors. You need to evaluate your current level of safety before creating a plan for this journey. Everyone has strengths as well as weaknesses, but writing them down has a larger impact than just thinking to yourself – "yes I have some weakness and strengths," and going on. What do you see as your weakness? What do you see as your strengths?

All of this comes with risk. A definition of risk is, "exposure to the chance of injury or loss; a hazard or dangerous chance" (dictionary.reference.com, 2016). In every single choice that is made, there is a chance of exposure to injury or loss, a hazard or something dangerous. I could stay in bed and there is a risk that the large dead branch on the tree outside could crash through the roof and mush me. Or I could get hit by an asteroid. I know it sounds weird, but the possibilities of anything happening are there. We take risks every single day, but measured in these risk that are taken, lies levels of risk and safety. The level of risk to stay in the bed and be hit by an asteroid is microscopic, but still there. Sometimes determining the level of risk a choice has is quite difficult, but many can be weighed without too much hardship.

To continue positive growth you will have to take risks, but taking on risks you are not prepared for can not only stagnate your planned journey but take you down some dark roads you do not need and do not want to venture. So a level of safety and level of risk should encompass your decisions and for the time, and it should be weighted more on the safety side. Many survivors have been dealing with negative issues from the assault(s) for so many years they want to jump in, move as fast as possible and put the past to rest. But if you do jump ahead and take risks you are not equipped to take, they can become setbacks and leave you feeling hopeless and frustrated. This is not some 6, 10, 20 session or week program and then you put down the book, print off some certificate that you now are healed, and go on with your life without any more issues or symptoms from experiencing MST. These are not steps to check off when finished, it is for the rest of your life, – a life plan. Now I am not saying that you need this book for the rest of your life, (let me puff up for a second and imagine it is used for at least a bunch of months). I am talking about the life plan you should make for yourself. It is like a map but not set in stone, it can be changed when necessary, but it will help you know where you want to go and the steps necessary to take you there. I hope this book is a springboard for that plan and for your journey, because it will take small steps, one at a time to get there.

It is recommended that you set the structure and pace for this journey. Trust your intuition when you begin to feel overwhelmed with any part of this book, or for that matter any part of your therapy. I have seen programs which push veterans into re-living their trauma; talking in extreme detail about it; asked to question themselves if it really could happen the way they "think" it did (and implant another reality); to talk in group when the person really did not want to; and one that irritates me so much – have the veteran falsely acknowledge any responsibility for the assault. I do not care what anyone has to say about believing there is any responsibility on the victim's part for the assault, there is NOT. I do not care what she: was wearing; not wearing; dinking; being in a restricted area; agreeing to take that offered ride; married; single; had a relationship with the perp; had talked about sex; joked about sex; bragged how many times she had sex; and I could go on and on. Again – the only responsibility for the assault was the perpetrator's CHOICE to assault you, nothing else caused it. I hear this a lot – "but she was not supposed to be drinking, she was underage, if she had not been drunk, she would not have been raped." Really? What limited use of a possible brain could ask this? Nobody knows what would or would not have happened, had she been drinking, or not. However, there is something that is known – he chose to do it, and had a choice to not.

Your safety is the priority, so at this time, are you in a safe place with people who can be counted on, to go further in this book (I do not use the word trust purposely – which I will discuss why under that subject)? Only you can answer that for yourself. If you are having trouble answering, here are some questions to ask yourself.

- Are you living with someone who physically hurts you in any way?
- Are you in a close relationship (boyfriend, friend, family member) with someone who hits objects (the wall) or throws objects, when they are upset?

- Do you find yourself continually taking inappropriate risks?
- Is someone close to you involved in illegal activities?
- Do you use any substances to drown your emotions – alcohol, drugs?
- Do you take more than the label states of any type of prescription medication (yours or someone else's)?
- Have you thought about suicide often? Do you have a plan? Do you have the means and aspiration to carry it out?
- Are you living with someone who verbally abuses you?
- Are you in a violent neighborhood?

The more questions you can answer yes to the above, the higher your level of risk is, but again – this is your choice to move forward. I ask only one thing from you at this point if you are thinking about hurting yourself – Please put down this book and call 1-800-273-8255.

Stress is not bad but a necessary part of facing life's challenges. Whilst the dreamers maintain the delusion that 'all accidents are preventable' the rest of us know that the bumps and challenges of life are necessary for learning, resilience and maturation. There can be no resilience without stress, and no learning without risk. - Dr Rob Long

---

Your Support System

Studies have shown survivors of trauma who have had a good support system fair significantly better than ones who do not. Who is in your support system? This is one of those better write it down than try and think through questions. A support system is not just people you have complete confidence in, that you can take anything to. A support system incorporates people, organizations, action plans and more. To be utilized for your ultimate potential. It can include the VA for your medical issues, medications and/or counselors; friends, who you can trust to speak only to about a specific topic; groups you can attend when you desire that extra boost; your religious leaders; family members who are supportive; and so forth. Every person or thing on the list has some specific type of positive helpfulness when needed. The more resources you seek out, the larger your network will grow.

You may never use some elements in your support system but that's okay, it is there if you need it, that's the purpose. Do not be discouraged if your system seems small, this is the time to realize that it is crucial for you to get more resources, so that if something occurs you will have someone (program, etc.), you can either get the help from or know who might have that information. At first you may feel hesitant to ask for help but we all need help. That's one reason we are here is to help one another. This list is not set in stone, others move off and some get more attached to them. Into the backpack.

Never assume that you can make it alone. You need the help of the Lord. Never hesitate to get on your knees in some private place and speak with Him. – Gordon B. Hinkley.

English Language = Oxymoron

The definition of language is the ability of one person to intelligibly communicate with another, but that is so far from what our language has become. Ever get a text message and think WTH (What the Hay)? After further messaging you now understand its true intent, which was far from what you thought it meant. That is one reason I like face to face conversations better. I can hear the tone of voice, see the body language and many times it takes what could have been construed as an insult, into what really was meant as a joke, you'd die laughing over. Someone could read the previous sentence and think that it is horrible and how could the death of anyone be funny – see the problem?

The words which we use on a daily basis, we know what we mean, but even if we do, not everyone around us does. Even after 24 years of marriage, I can tell my husband something and he receives it completely different. Even saying "listen to the words coming out of my mouth" does nothing since he is listening, it is the definitions of the words between us. That is the program.

Different regions have different meaning for words. There are many words which have more than one definition; and these definitions are sometimes nothing alike. The one I think about most is, two people are standing there, one yells, "Duck." The other looks around, "Where?" As he gets hits in the head by something. Duck – the bird, and duck - the movement, have nothing in common, but the right interpretation is very serious when trying to convey the message to get out of danger's way.

Just as deducing of the words which people, programs, and organizations, utilize, you should ascertain what they specifically imply to you. Write them down. Frequently when you write, you start to realize there is a more appropriate word, which more closely defines what you are trying to communicate.

*If the English language made any
sense, a catastrophe would be an
apostrophe with fur. – Doug Larson*

The Words We Chose to Use

The words we choose to use, the interpretations of them and our perception of them matters a great deal on this journey. We all use words, but I have exposed the choice of a person's words, their definitions, and their perceptions of them are not the same, even when describing the same situation. I absolutely loathe the English language. I did not when I was younger and writing my own personal fiction stories. I thought I was an awesome writer, then I got into high school. I took AP English, everyone else seemed to take it, so what was the deal? I had been talking and writing English my whole life, at least that was what I thought. When my first paper was returned it appeared to have been on the set of a B-rated murder scene in a horror show. I used math logic when speaking to the teacher. Me – "Did you understand what I said?" Teacher – "Yes?" Me – "So what's the problem?" My assumption was that correct grammar just meant the reader understood what had been written; I mean really, isn't that the whole reason for writing? Apparently that teacher, and no other English teacher after that agreed with me.

At times, I would rather some of the scientific articles I read used my math logic instead of using the thesaurus and finding archaic words last spoken during the 1800s. Or finding "comparable' words which have more letters in them than room on a line. When having to look up these words, nobody really uses in speech, I find numerous definitions, sometimes they have nothing to do with one another. I read a bunch of books, articles, and papers, and have gotten pretty good at choosing the correct explanation, that I believe the author intended to use. Then other times, I just guess.

With all that said, just as the dictionary has different definitions for the same word, people have different ones too. On top of that, some words become vogue but are used outside their true definition, it spreads and soon everyone is using a word in a completely wrong context, eventually that definition just gets added to the dictionary, (thanks).Word meanings do not just change over time, they change over location, over cultures, over sub-cultures and even down to specific families. There were 'swear words' in my family of origin that were not in my friend's households, and just the opposite.

Within this book, there are days when abstractions triumph, others I have a hard time remembering how to spell "of" and basic verbiage is all I can scribble, it mimics gobbledygook. I sanctioned a modification to my pharmaceuticals. After the third day of sluggishly tapering onto the desired dosage, I was revived from slumbering, and perceived a sensation that my brains and blood were oozing out. I ascertained for trauma, but acquired zilch. Merging in was an unfamiliar awareness, it resembled worms, wiggling around about my brain, fabricating their individual pathways. They refrained from devouring my gray matter, enjoying a rhapsodic occasion. I promptly ceased all hallucinatory medication. I toiled for three weeks to revert to my normal. I ogled at what I authored, it was cryptic. It materialized at the script of an unauthorized diacetylmorphine practitioner, which was horrifying. My capacity to fathom what I was undertaking, provoked an inquisition. It induced an impetus for publication. It produces the translucence of the maddening of my mind. As you have guessed, some days I write common, others I'm off on a psychedelic word ride. I trust it does not dismiss the material. And, at times, it was amusing to compose!

When talking about this subject, it is vital that everyone be on the same word page. When programs are created, laws written and etcetera, it is essential for definitions to be used, so that there is no guessing what was meant. In this book I write out many definition of words so that, hopefully, what I am trying to convey is received that way. I use the word – sexual assault, to mean rape, attempted rape, and certain types of sexual harassment. Sometimes I use the term – sexual assault to refer to mainly just rape, but hopefully have been clear in my writing around the word, that you will recognize what I mean. Typing sexual assault, sexual harassment, and rape, over and over makes long sentences which feel redundant, so I will shorten, at times, with just – sa/sh, which refers to sexual assault and/or sexual harassment.

What do these words mean to you? How do you define rape? Sexual assault? Sexual Contact? And Sexual Harassment? What words do you use to describe yourself? What words do you use to describe victims? How do you refer to the person accused of sexual assault and sexual harassment?

Comprehending how an agency or person defines certain terms allows you to realize their interpretations, towards the terms. In the military an easy way to dismiss an accusation of sexual assault is to utilize some definitions that are not in the UCMJ, even though the UCMJ is supposed to be the standard. When an agency, program or person uses "physical contact of a sexual nature" as part of the definition of sexual harassment only, it is assigning what truly is sexual assault into the sexual harassment category, taking it out of the criminal side. When commanders and persons in authority decide to make the victim believe what they experienced was not sexual assault, they scramble the definition, to be sexual harassment. It removes the report to another organization, essentially keeping it out of the reports for sexual assaults.

I hate to use the words – allegation, claimed, alleged, suspected, or suspect. These words have been purposely used to remove the responsibility from the perp and place it onto the victim; that she now must prove what happened. I actually had to look in the thesaurus because continually putting perpetrator was getting superfluous but there are just not that many words for these pervs. I get lambasted, how can I convict the guy, isn't he innocent until proven guilty? Actually no. I am not a court. I am validating the victim. Seriously, you listen to the facts of the cases, you know what happened, just because he got off on a technicality or was not charged because of the stupidness of command; he still did it. We are not stupid, not being convicted is not the same as being innocent.

I make it a point to refer to the person(s) who committed these acts as: perps, perpetrators, predator, assailants, jerk and/or bad guy. They do not get away with just being labeled: alleged suspect, supervisor, fellow soldier, etc. Using these terms allows others a deeper understanding and a conviction from me, that it was not a misunderstanding, it was purposeful and you and I know it.

Words have no power to impress the mind without the exquisite horror of their reality. – Edgar Allen Poe

---

No Two Veterans are Alike

I have been a veteran's advocate for decades and there have been understandably some common misconceptions among civilians about us but also among veterans. The Army is the largest of all the military branches, so it would be obvious the Army would have more numbers of veterans, and more numbers of MST survivors; however, we did not all join the Army. I say this because time and time again I come across veterans (sorry but especially the Army) and they begin to talk in their branch's jargon. All the branches share a lot of military terms, but there are terms that are not used among all the services. Along with some terms that actually mean something completely different between branches.

I do not have an MOS (Military Occupational Specialty), never did, I did not join the Army. The Air Force has AFSCs (Air Force Specialty Code). When my Army friends are asked what they do, they spill out some numbers, which actually do not mean anything to me, even though I am a veteran. If I get asked what I did in the military I say "Law Enforcement, K-9 Handler;" I have yet to come across someone who actually knew what my career code was (if I just said it – 81152a) except for some fellow security police, who has been in prior to its change. There no longer are Security Police. They are now called Security Forces.

While I was in, I was referred to as Airman, troop, and soldier. I utilize the word 'soldier' for all branches, because I was called it by other branch members. I never referred to any Air Force member above the Airman rank as Airman. Airman was a rank. All enlisted were referred to with their rank, as a group it was soldiers, officers were all sir or ma'am. That is how it was for me. It all depends on your branch of service, when you were in, what career field, where you were stationed and so much more as to how your military experience was, and the jargon you acquired. My son is in the Air Force now, he called the person he was buddied with in Basic Training –wingman, and they (as a whole) are all Airmen. It's a whole new Air Force.

Even if you were in the AF at the same time I was, same rank, same career, our experiences are so very different, in the details, but the same in the bigger picture. When talking with other veterans, please sympathize that they did not experience what you did and they may say "this wouldn't have happened" in their branch and/or job. I am here to tell you, you are not alone. It happens in all the branches, in all places, in all career field, to all ranks, to both women and men.

Civilian Luggage

There are many reasons people join the military. At first I saw an ability to prove I could do something that others said I could not. But after a little while, before actually going in, I saw it as an opportunity to do something I wanted to do. Some see the military as an escape from their current circumstances into something with more opportunities than they presently have. Others follow their family's tradition of service. Whatever the reason(s) a person decides to join, all have their own individual assumptions about how it will be, and a lot of it can turn out to be very wrong.

What were your reasons for joining? What were some of your assumptions? How many were correct? Which ones are you totally laughing about now?

Do you remember your Basic Training? Boot Camp? Let's go to my 'fictitious' Basic Training. I watched what most brought and dumped out on their bed for our security check. Put what would was not necessary, or was not allowed in its proper place; medications taken and disposed of or kept by the TI; most clothing put away for Basic; and what little we could keep had to fit in the top security drawer in our wall lockers. I remember two very distinctive persons and their items. The one right down from my bunk was the first to be verbally attacked by our male TI. I did not know what she had expected Basic to be like but it seemed she had gathered most of her stuffed animals and put them into her luggage. Maybe a sleep-away camp? A bunch of girls together in bunks playing military games? Maybe she had other branch friends or family members that told her the Air Force wasn't really a military. She had a four-piece matching luggage set stuffed with all you would desire – curling iron, blow dryer, bunches of makeup, even night rollers, material for nails, and I think I even saw paraphernalia for pedicures. And a zoo of stuffed animals. Now I had stuffed animals, but I did not bring them to Basic. I wouldn't have dared.

The other person was in the other bay, but everyone could hear almost all of the 'discussion' she was having with first our female TI, who then called the male over for help. Her friends had thought it would be a funny joke to put condoms, lots of them, all through all her suitcases. Both of them arrived with civilian luggage, but they came from different parts of the country and actually different worlds.

Before even joking about joining the military I wanted to be a police officer and when I found out that the military would allow me to be one, once I graduated technical school, I knew what I wanted to do. I wanted to protect and serve. My assumptions of the military and especially my career field, was completely unrealistic. I thought law enforcement would be full of honest people who wanted to protect and serve like I did. I assumed since the military had tons of policy, procedures, codes and regulations and a facade of honor, that even if someone wanted to be evil or self-serving all the rules would keep them from doing it.

I have yet to meet any person who didn't have any afflictions in their family growing up. I have met families which loved each other dearly. Fathers which came home and helped with chores, loved their wives and children, you would think the perfect family, yet even they had problems. Not what many would call problems, but we all have our own and at very different levels. They were what some consider normal life infirmities, the semi-rebellious (but not too much) teenage years, some (but not a lot) financial difficulties, but over all, their children had wonderful childhoods. Others are TV Reality shows for how not to be a parent; absent fathers; abusive mothers; mothers bring home pedophile boyfriends and wonder why they rape her children; fathers who rape their children; fathers who beat on their wives; parents who are drug users and prostitute out their children for drugs; alcoholic fathers who beat then kick out their children; alcoholic mothers who are too drunk to see that their children are getting hurt by their alcoholic friends; and everything in between.

When talking about military experiences, many people focus on just what happened during that time as if the first 18 years of that person's life was eventless. Do not think that I am saying, having had been traumatized prior to the military, that somehow there is a looming aura of victimness around you. Just realize what you went into the military with, should be addressed along with the experiences within the military. I came in not trusting many people, but being very naive, and somewhat sheltered did not help. As it happens for many, my high school friends grew apart from me, I was pretty much on my own dealing with anything.

Although we all went through Basic/Boot Camp, we came in with different attitudes, different experiences, and our own individual physical, mental and emotional civilian luggage. This does not in any way, give any responsibility of the assault to you. Again that completely falls on the perpetrator, but nobody came in naked, even if it was just in civilian clothes on their backs. We all had civilian luggage.

What civilian luggage did you take in with you?

3

WHAT IS MST?

You Are Not Alone

I never asked if I was the only one suffering. Unfortunately, I knew I was not because I saw victims get revictimized from the very people who were supposed to "protect and serve." During my initial Law Enforcement Technical School training, I was taught there were no victims, everybody was considered a suspect. When it came to any sexual crime or physical assault against women, it was not looked at as "criminal." Most of the guys who I worked with had the attitude that she somehow had done something that caused her to become a victim. Victims were branded weak.

When dealing with people, they were placed into a hierarchal order. In the states it was first military then civilians. In Panama, people were on a larger hierarchy of worth: hookers on the bottom; then regular civilians; non-US military; US civilians and last US military. Investigative techniques used against a victim were no different from questioning someone you thought committed a crime: "What were you doing there?"; "Why did you go?"; "Were you drinking?"; "What were you wearing?"; "What did you say to him?" And the one most never expect, unless you have been in that situation. "Are there are witnesses to your story?" The reason for the last question was twofold. The first part was questioned because if there was a witness, we might get the "real story." The second part of the question was used because we were taught most all of these cases were just that, stories. It was utterly inappropriate and reprehensible, we were trained that way and it was reinforced on the job.

The Department of Veterans Affairs seemly coined the term Military Sexual Trauma; however, the limitation of its first definition, and the continual changing of the definition, prompted me to make an official one of my own. Many mistakenly believe that within Public Law 102-585, or even Chapter 17 of Title 38 lies the legal definition of military sexual trauma. But the term is never used in the law. Although it has provisions for people who are given access to counseling and other services, there is no definition.

On the website, the latest official VA definition of military sexual trauma is:

"Military sexual trauma, or MST, is the term used by VA to refer to experiences of sexual assault or repeated, threatening sexual harassment that a Veteran experienced during his or her military service. The definition used by the VA comes from Federal law (Title 38 U.S. Code 1720D) and is "psychological trauma, which in the judgment of a VA mental health professional, resulted from a physical assault of a sexual nature, battery of a sexual nature, or sexual harassment which occurred while the Veteran was serving on active duty, active duty for training, or inactive duty training." Sexual harassment is further defined as "repeated, unsolicited verbal or physical contact of a sexual nature which is threatening in character" (va.gov, 2016).

The definition I utilize is unlike the VA's in that theirs is fickle, politically driven, ever changing, not one derived from education, experiences, facts and/or understanding. MST includes physical and verbal attacks. Because both are within the definition, a sexual assault is physical, therefore the trauma experienced, cannot only be limited to psychological, as in the VA's definition.

Military Sexual Trauma is the experience of sexual assault or sexual harassment, resulting in an immediate or long-term, physical or psychological injury, which occurred while the person was on active duty, in the U.S. Armed Forces.

Sexual assault is any type of sexual contact that occurs without the explicit consent of the recipient. The definition of sexual harassment for the above is: repeated, unsolicited verbal or physical contact of a sexual nature which is threatening in character. This MST definition is without political agendas, not catering to counseling programs nor healthcare, or the access to healthcare. It is regardless of: sex; veteran status, discharge condition, judgement of a mental health professional; however this definition is solidified. I do not agree with the addition of "active duty for training" or "inactive duty for training." Active duty for training is already included as "active duty." Active duty is just that, full-time active duty. "Inactive duty for training" was added for healthcare access and doesn't have to be. Access can be granted without weakening the definition of the term to something that is not the same. The continual broadening of the definition lowers the efficacy of the research with the unique conditions MST encompasses and reduced its significance as a distinctive category. This does not disregard victims who were on inactive duty and sexually assaulted or sexually harassed; it merely separates them as does the two terms "date rape" and "acquaintance rape" are separate terms with distinctive definitions.

Normal Responses
Some common emotional, physical and psychological reactions:
- Abandonment
- Aggression
- Anger

- Anxiety (panic attack)
- Avoidance (of people, places or things)
- Begin or increased use/abuse of alcohol or drugs (illegal, prescription, over-the-counter)
- Betrayal
- Changes in appetite
- Denial
- Depression
- Detachment
- Difficulty in remembering parts or the entire trauma
- Difficulty concentrating
- Difficulty trusting
- Disbelief
- Disoriented or out of touch with reality
- Embarrassment
- Fear
- Feeling out of control
- Feelings of helplessness
- Flashbacks
- Guilt
- Headaches
- Homicidal thoughts with or without a plan
- Hallucinations
- Hypervigilance
- Irritability
- Isolation
- Loss of intimacy
- Loss of periods of time
- Need to control
- Nightmares
- Not being able to stop thinking about the incident
- Numbness
- Self-blame

- Self-Harm
- Shame
- Shock
- Sleeplessness
- Spiritual crisis
- Stomach aches
- Stress
- Suicidal Ideation with or without a plan
- Unable to experience joy or love

Understanding Trauma

Trauma is more difficult when the tragedy is cause by people rather than natural disasters. Traumas such as rape, sexual abuse, or threat to personal life are identified with people. The victim is left with a severely reduced ability to trust (network54. com).

There are two kinds of trauma – physical and mental. Physical trauma is the body's response to the physical injury, usually to a severe degree. Mental or Psychological trauma refers to fear-provoking thoughts and painful feelings. Both traumas can cause real physical pain. However, the term "traumatic experience" refers to a trauma which was out of the ordinary experience of most people, life-threatening, which occurred to you, or that you witnessed the incident. Sexual assault IS a traumatic experience, as can be sexual harassment.

The resiliency of a person, when discussing trauma, can be visualized like a rubber band. The person is stretched during the trauma; however, the more the rubber band continually is stretched, the less the bouncing back happens, it can cause less resilience. Each person starts as a different rubber band – with diverse genetic makeup; some are just more resilient than others. Newer, youthful rubber bands generally have better overall rubberability than older ones. But the more traumatic experiences a person experiences the more residual effects they'll have.

Will I ever feel the same? This question has been asked and pondered by millions and the answer is no. No, you will never feel the same. It would be asinine to believe that anyone could completely delete any traumatic experience from their life. That is the definition of life - all our experiences, good and bad. The past is just that, in the past and cannot be changed. This is not to say that the symptoms which are present now will continue, but you have experienced military sexual trauma, and that trauma cannot be erased. Even though it cannot be eliminated it is not a sentence for a life of misery. You can become a Thriver. A Thriver is someone who progresses beyond just surviving the experience; they begin to thrive with life. You can once again experience: joy, happiness, fulfillness, love, pleasure, purpose, a sense of connectedness, honor, trust, respect, pride, self-value and a positive self-image. You alone can begin to take charge of your life, begin to empower yourself and find the light at the end of the darkness. This beginning of this process is reaching out to others, ask for help. Find like-minded individuals and others who have also experienced military sexual assault.

For every person who enters this journey they bring assumptions as to what healing, healed, recovery and recover are. These words are difficult to define in terms of sexual assaults. What one person views as recovery or healing, another does not. A simplistic example, all major cuts to the body are wounds, injuries which demand aid. What type and degree of aid depends on many factors: how deep the wound is; where the wound is located; what was used to make the wound; how much blood is coming out and other variables. Once the specific life-threatening aid to the wound has been rendered then healing can begin. The healing process can be a degree of additional aids (surgery, stitches, medication), but in all cases action must be taken. You cannot allow the injury to go without assistance or it will become infected. Some people's wounds will heal faster than others, some will leave larger scars, but all have been injured. Major obstacles in the healing process can be: pretending as though the wound is not there; ignoring all the pain; having the wound reopened; the wrong type of medication; self-medicating the pain away with alcohol or drugs; being around toxic people who will infect the wound; not following the prescribed care; and any number of other influences. These influences will slow down, stop, or reverse the healing process. Along with taking care of the wound, you must be kind to the rest of the body to allow ample energy to be focused on that area.

There is no one way anyone will respond to any traumatic experience, just as there is no one way you should have responded; the when or if these responses occur is just as variant. Each person will respond in time and reaction to their own unique experience(s), in their own particular time, and in their own individual ways. These reactions may last for several hours, days, weeks, months, and even years; they can be mild, moderate or severe. Accept that you are not going nuts, losing your mind, or going off the deep end. You have experienced a sexual trauma which is a traumatic event. Your reactions are normal and there is no shame in them. You are normally reacting to an out of the normal event.

All the parts of our bodies are connected in one fashion or another, what happens to one part can (affect) the others. Because of this, sa/shs are injuries to the mind, to the body and to the soul. Trying to fix one injury, while ignoring the others, will leave the rest to fester and grow. To recover or heal, the entire Self needs to be kept in mind.

You find yourself in the park and suddenly a bear breaches the bushes- what do you do? Fight? Flight? Do you puff up, yelling and pretend you are bigger and badder than the bear – fight? Do you exit stage left as fast as possible – flight? Or maybe you just stand there – freeze? I have heard many ask victims, "Why didn't you do anything?" Others blame – "if it really was a sexual assault, why didn't you fight or run away?" Then there is people who have never been in the situation, "I'd fight it out," "I'd run," "but I would never just let it happen." I do not remember letting, as in agreeing to, or allowing anyone do that, and I don't except anyone else would either. In the animal world, when an opossum is threatened, one of its survival techniques is to play dead. I have an inclination they don't assess the situation – "I think I could take this fox" or "I'm close to that hole, I can make it." No, this is an automatic survival response. You never go through the exact same trauma. Nobody knows how they will respond during an assault until it happens to them. Many may say they will react in a specific way, but find out that when it happens; they do not. There can be extremely similar circumstances, but it can never be the same. So each trauma is a new experience.

So what determines which response will be mobilized? Let's go back to our wonderful, numerous, variables, oh so many. There is the chemical activation, and the response. You can be trained to automatically respond in a specific way when being attacked.

You can even train your brain, and that's what you are essentially doing. I do not mean the thought side, but the automatic side. There are many different regions of the brain that are impacted by trauma. Some of the chemicals will help with strength, for the ability to fight or flee; while other chemicals are going to deaden your pain receptacles. The flight or fight is missing another f- freeze. When an overabundance of certain chemicals enter the body, a documented automatic neurobiological condition called toxic immobility, can happen. This is not something the victim has decided to do. There is no thought process along with it. A person in this state literally cannot move, she is essentially paralyzed. The victim did not decided to freeze. Before any thought processes happened chemicals flooded the body and determined how she would react.

God will take you as you are at this very moment and begin to work with you. All you need is a willing heart, a desire to believe, and trust in the Lord. – Dieter F. Uchtdorf

---

Feelings

I have heard people over and over sing the first part of the song, by Morris Albert, "Feelings, nothing more than feelings." I wondered why they only sang the first part, until I heard the rest of it and then appreciated it was only that fragment. But thinking of the song, it is just that, nothing more than feelings. They are not right, not wrong, or even true; they just are. They also are not facts. Your feelings are produced by first a thought or trigger, which is transferred into an emotion which releases chemicals, then transmutes into a feeling. How you react to the feeling is your behavior. I had to wrap my head around this one, and yes it did cause a headache. So I surfed the internet, pulled out dozens of my personal library books, dragged through dozens of scientific articles, and discovered many had conflicting wording with similar definitions. Some used 'emotions' and 'feelings' interchangeably, others were extremely adamant about their distinction. I can see and comprehend the necessity for the division.

While I was wrapping my head around this concept, I thought about how I would explain this, and pulled from my school days.

On the playground at my school there was this high metal slide, unless you stopped at the top and readjusted yourself you would end up at the bottom, on your face. So think about my school playground slide. You are at the bottom and begin to climb. The beginning is the trigger, or the thought. Quickly, within less than a second, your body replies by producing chemicals which head out into the rest of the body. This is an emotion, the physical release of specific chemicals caused by the trigger and/or the thought. As you ascend the ladder you begin to feel, whether it is anxiety, fear, or excitement, but you begin within yourself to sense, a feeling. There is something different from a second ago when you were standing on the ground. Your heart begins to race, your hands are sweaty, breathing more shallow, this is the chemicals being pumped into your system. You're at the top and can quickly fling yourself onto the slide; pause and allow the feelings to deepen or diminish, with some more thoughts; or slightly readjust, close your eyes and push off.

The struggle is in the way we talk about: feelings, thoughts, emotions, emotional responses, and behaviors. We use these words to mean things that are not the same. You say you feel angry, but this can come from a thought or trigger, and since anger is a secondary emotion, sometimes you cannot easily figure out what the primary one is. Especially when you have been trained to move all of them into anger. To actually know what the first thought or trigger was and then to name the first accompanying emotion along with it can be problematic. To me, I subscribe to the distinction, but in everyday language is sounds weird and confusing. I know the variation but when normally talking, all of them are jumbled up. I could try and sort through them and make sure I was using what I should, but it takes away from the intimaceness of how I want this book to feel. So I put this in the book, to allow you the knowledge to know the particularities, but just as I stated about the English language, it's terrible and convoluted, but I am just going to go with it.

Essentially to be able to change the feeling you have to change your thoughts, but also cope with the triggers, which are not thought-first based. To change the thought, you have to know what that thought is, and be able to stop on the up on the slide before the emotional chemicals run through your body and you just go with it. Or to counteract that emotion with another thought to cancel it out or override it. After being able to identify your thought, the trigger, or the feeling, you can pause - halt somewhere before you go down the slide head first. It is not an easy process, you have had years of just going along with whatever is happening, to reacting to what may seemed to have been out of your control. The tendency to not control these can be challenging to really believe there is thoughts and perceptions of senses, behind all of this. So you are not a failure when you slide, it is habitual and will take time to retrain your brain, and retrain your automatic responses.

Feelings of worth come when a woman follows the example of the Master. Her sense of infinite worth comes from her own Christlike yearning to reach out with love, as He does. Russell M. Nelson

---

Triggers

In psychological terminology the word trigger is normally used to define a trauma trigger and not just an ordinary trigger. A trauma trigger is something which fires off memories or causes a flashback of a previous traumatic event. This term, as with so many others, has been so misused most do not grasp the true impact of a bona-fide trauma trigger.

You walk into a bakery shop and the sweet smell of freshly baked bread engulfs your body. You remember the bread your grandmother used to bake with you. As you continue to purposely, happily, recall your memories, you can see her smiling face with sprinkles of flour dusting her hair. A warmth comes to your body and you decide, with a smile, fresh baked bread, has now been added to your list. The smell of the bread was a trigger, but not the trauma trigger of the psychological type, within the definition that includes 'flashbacks' and 'traumatic events.' It can be usefully to intentionally distinguish the two in your writing and speech by using t-trigger, trauma trigger or traumatic trigger; whichever one you like better.

On a daily basis we can have thousands of triggers. I do not believe I go one day without my spider trigger getting switched. My husband laughs when we sit on the couch and I point to the other side of the room, on an ornate oriental carpet, and say "spider." We've been together for 24 years and he still gets up and walks over to check out the assumed spider. Sure enough, when he gets his face down almost touching the carpet, he sees the microscopic spider 'waiting to kill' (my perception, my reality. Really, you know that is what that little bugger is up to).

My spider triggers are not little dust balls or pieces of hair; they are either actual spiders, or must be at least ½ inches in diameter, roundish with 'legs,' and dark brown or black in color. I associate that to my tours in Panama. Although, I do at times jump, my heart does race, they are not on my traumatic trigger list, but they used to be. Some triggers have never been on my list, only because of my perception of the incident. This is where you define what your traumatic triggers are; however, do not condemn yourself if you are triggered and cannot seem to pinpoint what the trigger is. Some take time, and some I have never figured out. They still are triggers, but nevertheless, I have developed positive coping skills for them.

I used, and believed it is the best, a traumatic trigger journal (a notebook if you prefer that term). It can be a little book that goes into your purse, or pocket; or an electronic one on your phone, watch, PC, or tablet. If you know what the trigger was, after you have completed your positive coping skill(s), jot it down. Also quickly note your impressions and physical responses, and a description of the area, time of day, day of week, etc.; like a draft novel (the main details are there, but not in such flowery wording). Here's the thing – you can believe that one item (smell, sound, sight, touch, taste), is a t-trigger, when actually there is a combination of them going on. Not writing them down, and just focusing on one, can make the other slip off, until it alone comes out and you're baffled. You cope with the one but keep getting triggered and can't figure it out.

Using my spider trigger – the quick glance is a trigger. Movement is a compounded trigger. Movement that is quickly heading toward me is death, and there has been thousands of faux spider deaths. Had I not been writing down my reactions, the time of day, if it was actually a spider, how big was it, what color, how and if it was moving. I would not know all the details of my spider trigger. You can stop laughing at any moment because I actually am trying to go somewhere with this. Dealing with the issue of a spider trigger, when and only when, I have actually spied a spider, is not dealing with the t-trigger. It was a spider that hurt me (ended up in a hospital bed because of one); but it was where the spider incidents were, the sizes, the colors, the movement, the shapes, how I saw them (out of the corner of my eye). Any one of those, early on, could be a t-trigger. People heard I hated spiders, but if it was not a spider, or was not a poisonous spider, they would discount my reaction, dismissing my t-trigger. Telling me to "Calm down. It is just a little harmless spider." In my mind, I knew there were harmless spiders but my t-triggers and survival responses (avoidance of pain), kicked in long before any logical thought construction could start. In effect, I was being condemned for something which occurred before I could even think.

Sleep

One of the most listed symptoms after an assault is insomnia, which can lead to sleep deprivation, and as some of the different articles suggested, sleep deficiency. I like the separation of these two words; that sleep deprivation is when you are not getting enough sleep, and sleep deficiency encompasses much more. Sleep deficiency is:

- Sleep deprivation.
- Do not sleep well, getting through all the stages.
- And/or sleep at the wrong time of day for your body's natural clock.

It is imperative for you to get the right amount of sleep, and the right amount of undisturbed sleep. Sleep occurs in cycles, if completed undisrupted it ranges from 90 to 110 minutes. There is scientific 'discussion' about the number of actual stages of sleep in the cycle. Although extremely interesting to me, after about a dozen or so articles and a few studies (yea, read them all), I like the four stage cycle the best. The first stage you can be easily awaken from, which can feel somewhat like falling, and at times you can hear things that are not there; like the sound of the doorbell or someone calling your name. The second is when your heart begins to slow down and your temperature lowers. Third stage is a transitional stage between light and very deep sleep where Delta Waves, deeper slower brain waves begin to emerge. The fourth is the well-known REM (rapid eye movement) stage. Although your brain and body systems become more active your muscles are more relaxed. This is where you typically dream at.

Problems with getting the right sleep - amount of time needed, going through the normal stages, and at the right time of day; can cause havoc on your mind and body. We have all had that night where we just cannot seem to get to sleep then finally do, but have to wake up early, at the same time for the next day. You can feel as though you have been ran over by a truck. People tell you things and a second later you are asking them "what?" Concentration diminishes, ability to respond slows, thought processes are sail-like; you get there but it takes longer and with more energy. Having a sleep problem and a night of bad sleep is very different. Sleep problems are sleep deprivation and deficiency; whereas, just not getting one or a few good night's sleep is just that. Sleep problems accumulate and increase in symptoms the more often they happen and the more they happen in sequence (night after night after night).

In the military there were plenty of times that I had to stay up for more than 24 hours. One of those times, I was up for three days, and my ability to function was seriously diminished. I did the close of the eyes, the head dipping and snap back to awake, shaking my head, as though I could shake off my body screaming it craved sleep. After I had a much needed good night's sleep, I sprang back to being ready. The most harm (that I felt and saw) was when I could not get enough undisturbed sleep. When I started to get little bits of sleep, here and there, it was a dissimilar feeling, altered inability to function. There was no bouncing back after an appropriate night's sleep, it took much longer, and unfortunately during that time there were not consistently good sleep nights.

Look back at what you did hours before it was bedtime. Did you down some soda? Coffee? Stock up on your sugar storage? Exercise? Watch something disturbing? Take medication to get to sleep? Many have noticed patterns of negative activities, which would disrupt anyone, let alone someone who is suffering with nightmares or insomnia. Once you can pinpoint a possible hindrance you can take action upon it.

Although many think that taking naps during the day helps out when you are having problems with sleep, this is not advised. If you take naps during the day, that actually disrupts your night time ability to sleep, as well as interfering with your sleep cycle. Most naps do not allow the body to get into a deep REM state, and this state is necessary, along with the other stages for optimal functioning.

There are many things that can be done to help you get a good night's sleep. And many things to avoid because they are obstacles. Have a sleep log and use it to write down what you do before you go to bed. How much sleep did you get? Did you wake up? How many times? Why did you wake up? Bathroom? Nightmare? Sound? Do you feel rested in the morning? Was there something you thought or felt that you could not seem to shake off? Write it all down. Keep this by your bed and after a week you can begin to see if you have patterns or problems which interrupt a good night's sleep. Try what you think will help. Adjust accordingly.

Here are some examples to help, while others are hindrances.
- Pray.
- Alcohol. You might be tricked into thinking this causes you to be drowsier and fall asleep faster, well it decreases your much needed REM sleep time, and adds other problems into your life.
- Breathing exercises.
- Do not read or watch anything scary, prior to sleep.
- Drinking lots of water will cause you to wake up and have to use the bathroom.

- Drink some herbal tea (not black or green but herbal tea).
- Eating chocolate, especially dark chocolate, will keep you awake. Okay, yes I know, and I do have problems with this, but I rationalize that it is milk chocolate.
- Get off the computer or any other device (tablet, phone, game) about three hours prior. There are studies coming out now, that the light from these electronic devices disrupts sleep as well as other negative aspects.
- Get up at the same time every day, even weekends, even if you did not get the amount or quality of sleep.
- Have a sleep routine. By having a sleep routine it begins to train your mind to move into that process when the routine starts. A sleep routine consists of a pattern of things you do and say to help you sleep. It can start hours before the time you actually want to sleep.
- Have fresh bedding.
- If you have not fallen asleep within 20 minutes get out of bed and do something, then try again.
- Listen to relaxing music.
- Mindfulness, meditation. Practice just feeling your surroundings, letting all thoughts come in, no judgement, no pausing, and let the thoughts flow out.
- No caffeine 6 hours prior to sleep.
- No heavy exercising.
- Reading or watching anything which reminds you of the trauma is not helpful (the news is terrible for this).
- Read something inspirational.
- Read the scriptures.
- Resist taking certain medications.
- Spicy or a big meal a few hours before bedtime is horrible on sleep as well as the tummy. I sometimes refer to this as The Taco Toss – flopping around feeling stuffed.
- Stretch your body, light stretching.

- Take a warm bath or shower. – I do not like baths, never did, so this is not at all relaxing to me. And I get energy and am ready to go after a shower, so that doesn't help either.
- Tighten your muscles (now this is not exercising, more of tightening your muscles and then releasing them). – I also use this one when my legs feel jumpy and just do not want to be still. I squeeze the leg muscles, hold, and then release.
- Turn down the thermostat. I love the heat, but I do, and most do also, sleep better when it is a little cooler.
- Try not to go over everything you need to do for the next day (unless it is to write it down and put it to bed also).
- Turn off your Facebook – I know I already mentioned the computer thing, but this is added on top of it. If you ever want to shake your head at the ignorance of humans, troll your Facebook. It does not have to be your friend, but you always seem to have that one friend who keeps the weirdest company, which can leak onto your screen and keep you up.
- Use a worry, problem, or thought journal to write down anything that is running through your mind, to put it to bed.
- Use the bedroom only for sleep (and sex with your husband).
- Worrying whether you checked all the locks, the windows or the oven keeps your mind awake. If this occurs put into your routine, a checklist of the things you normally check more than once. When you check it, put the date and the time. Keep it by your bed in case you are like me and sometimes forget what I had done right before walking into the bedroom. During the day make a list out. If you think you didn't do something, all you have to do is look at your list.

Sleep is that golden chain that ties health and our bodies together. – Thomas Dekker

Safety Again

We are back to safety again. I cannot stress how important this subject is for your positive journey. In Maslow's hierarchy of needs, it lists safety right above the physiological essentials; using the simplistic aspect – water, food, and rest. Once your physical necessities have been secured, safety is next. Your mind cannot properly focus when you are fixated on your own safety. This is not selfish, it is survival mode. Before you can move your attention to thoughts of love and belonging, it is essential for the safety method to be addressed.

You have the right to protect yourself, your physical and mental self, from all abuse. If you are in a relationship which is abusive, do not kid yourself into thinking that you are going to change the other person, or that any amount of abuse is okay, "as long as that other person" - stays around, pays the bills, is the child's father, is a relative, says they are going to change, is providing housing and/or anything else. You have the right to not be physically or mentally abuse in anyway, by ANYONE!

Most MST survivors have had their sense of safety shattered. Getting back a level that you can feel comfortable with sometimes is not that easy. There are many things that we do not have control over in this world, but when you have the choice to lessen the risk, it is always something to ponder. Trust your gut instinct. After an assault many (and I did this too) question whether or not their own judgement can be trusted. You might have thought you were good at reading people, knowing what they were up to, but now you question everything. If there is a question, always caution on the safety side. I would rather be called wicked than dead.

There are so many safety checklists and suggestions on the internet, research them. A much missed safety component is the internet. My husband, Dr. Doug Wells, wrote a book, *Social Self-defense,* discussing that very subject. If you went to your social media account and searched what your fiends have posted, how many of them are putting out so much information they have heightened their risk? Many don't think anything about telling everyone that they'll be on vacation for a week, when their spouse is on a business trip, or on deployment. Not just what you say, but how many pictures can you put together to be able to have a layout of your house and the yards?

With all the information we have available to us, it can get a little alarming to know how easy that can get into the wrong hands. Children especially do not comprehend the evil people trolling the web. This is why it is essential to focus on our safety. And being cautious is not paranoid, it is being careful. With that, here are a few of the ones I got off the net after a few minutes-

- You can take self-defense classes.
- Practice your military training.
- When driving lock all your doors and roll up your windows.
- Get a dog and make sure that it is trained.
- Change things up. Predictability can be hazardous.
- Get off the phone. I see so many people whose full attention is on their phone. Whether it is walking down the street, sitting in the car, or even driving. It has become an electronic pacifier.
- When moving into a new place, or when spending the night at a hotel, look at the vents. Especially the smoke

detectors, to see if someone has placed a camera in there. This should be accompanied with changing out the locks, of your new place.

- Use the buddy system when going out. If you are going out with a bunch of women, make sure you all come back. There is no guy worth the risk to leave with.

- I am an enormous advocate of not drinking at all, but if you are going to drink, do not get drunk. There is such a high association with alcohol and sexual assault it is not worth it.

A prudent man foreseeth the evil, and hideth himself: but the simple pass on, and are punished. - Proverbs 22:3

4

COPING STRATEGIES

All of us who have ever been afraid, nervous, anxious, tense, jumpy or edgy, have coping strategies. Coping strategies are behavioral, physical, and mental instruments to help counterbalance or conquer thoughts and feelings. Most use the term defense mechanisms as the negative and coping skills to be the positive sides.

There are thousands of positive activities you can do plus there are techniques (e.g., visualization, breathing techniques) you can learn when you do not have the opportunity to leave a situation without serious consequences. Remember you probably have been using defense mechanisms for years. So it will take conscious thought and practice to be able to catch yourself before the automatic kicks in and to retrain your brain. Trying to just eliminate a learned behavior usually does not work, you have to replace that negative behavior with a positive one.

You should explore if what you are doing is nourishing you mentally, physically and spiritually. Are you automatically drawn to coping skills or defense mechanisms?

Coping Skills

- Control breathing techniques
- Count to 100 by 3's
- Do a cross word puzzle
- Engage in a hobby
- Exercise
- Figuring out a puzzle
- Looking over your "Happy Journal" or "Funny Journal"

- Meditating
- Playing a board game
- Pray
- Read the funnies
- Reading a book
- Reading the Scriptures
- Recreational activities
- Sing a hymn
- Stretching
- Swimming
- Taking a bath
- Taking a leisurely walk
- Visualize your "safe place"

Defense Mechanism

Which of these defense mechanisms have you used?

- Abusing food
- Abuse of over-the-counter medications
- Alcohol
- All or nothing thinking
- Emotional reading
- Denial
- Drug abuse
- Labeling
- Learned helplessness
- Negative filtering
- Numbing
- Overeat
- Physically destructive behavior (nail biting, cutting)
- Psychic reading
- Running away
- Unrealistic expectations

Purposeful Life

The military's mission, as a whole, is to defend the US and US interests. Each branch has its own specific part of the whole. The further down in structure, the more specific, but everyone has a mission, a purpose for being there. Yes, I do remember walking around in circles with no real purpose for the day, other than being annoyed; but the main purpose never changed. At any time I could be pulled out to do what I was trained for. I was a part of something much more than myself, and much more than just the people I worked with on a daily basis. It had a sense of closeness, belonging (to a point), but also pride. I was proud of serving my country.

Every day I woke up, the mission was always there. It was comforting to know what you would be doing (pretty much so). A sense of knowing that I really mattered, that what I did really mattered. It can be hard after having such a distinct and vital purpose to come back and have people want you to staple papers because they do not know what your skills really are.

My main purpose in life is to get to Heaven and help as many other people obtain that destination also, and that has never changed. But when I got out of the service, I felt lost. I stumbled around and finally began to map out what I wanted along the way to my life's goal; through mini goals. These mini goals, like any goal are thought out, written down, planned and prayed about. Without planning, it is just a dream and I might or might not reach it. But with it mapped out, I know where I am heading. These mini goals can morph or even be completely changed, but they all are written down, and prayed about.

I am okay with my place. My mini goals changed, which change is at times frightening, but the main life goal will never change. What are your mini goals? Finding a purpose to get up in the morning can seem to be daunting. I spent a long time searching out different non-profits, I thought I could work with. So far none have panned out to my specific criteria, so I created one – GI Joan Project. It has been added onto my other mini goals, of which I seem to have amassed a lot of them, but it keeps me busy. I do make a difference and that is very satisfying. If I can help just one more woman veteran, then all the work is worthwhile.

Everyone has the potential for greatness. Not fame, money, degrees, and/or statutes made; but actual greatness - helping out another person, making a difference in their life for the better. Helping others is wonderful; however, trying to help when you're not in a situation to, does not work out well. You may want to jump in and help out other veterans, women veterans, women and/or MST survivors. But until you know what most your triggers are and have developed the coping skills to manage the symptoms, staying away from possible triggers is best. It can take a while to find a match to your skills, wants and an organization's needs, but there is a multitudinous (myriad, numerous) of them to choose from.

Some would love, and do, not have to work but still bring in money. I am not one of them. I have always liked to be an asset to society, do something worthwhile. When my children were younger, it was the full-time mom, and it is the best job. There is no job more invaluable, when you have children, then to be the one to raise them. Raising happens all the time, not after 5pm. They are such precious gifts from Heaven. I taught my children the joy of service. We volunteered for many noteworthy organizations. I wrote about women veteran's issues, and specifically military sexual trauma.

Only 4 years ago I began to get out from behind the keyboard and help veterans in person. It worked for a while, until I came upon an evil woman who was pathologically jealous of my accomplishments and the non-profit which cared less about the lives of veterans. Since then, I have reformed that mini goal. With all my other issues, having to go anywhere to speak, is complicated. Can't do the 9-5. After I attended VWise, it solidified what I was already doing that it could be something more. So I did. I started some home-based businesses to accomplish the mini goal of service.

I have had many businesses in the past, and felt I could help others have a little extra income in their life, as well as supplement my income to be able to help other women veterans and MST survivors. All the money that I make goes toward women veterans and MST survivors. I have several mini-businesses, but each one is specific for different items. My main website is *–JustCrafty.com*. This is where you can click over to my other businesses, see other books I have written, my Battle Buddies, the jewelry (with my MST ribbon on) plus the other ones I created, and all sorts of other enjoyable products.

One of those businesses, the company Melaleuca, it is a great company. I found it searching for cleaning supplies which I could actually use. After I was exposed to whatever it was in Saudi, I have not been able to be around most cleaning supplies without getting physically sick. Melaleuca is an eco-friendly company which has more than just cleaning supplies. It carries vitamins, make-up, soap, shampoo, weight-loss supplies and so much more. I use the vitamins and just love them.

Again, from Saudi and Panama I no longer have a goat stomach. I have to be very careful what I do eat, and it has been a battle trying to find good healthy food in the store. I came across this company – *Thrive Life*. It has freeze-dried foods. I use it on a daily basis, and stock up on my food storage (in case of emergencies). I really like that I only use the amount that I need. My children are off to college and the Air Force, and currently (maybe not by the time this is published), my husband lives in another city. Cooking for teenagers and then cooking for one is so very different. There is not a whole lot of single packaging that is not laced with tons of salt and other non-pronounceable words. If I want ½ a cup of ground beef, or ¼ of a cup, I can now just get it out. No thawing and then tossing any away, or trying to figure out what else I can have the next day, with ground beef. If you want to learn more about Thrive Life, just click over from my JustCrafty.com site.

Melaleuca has great make-up, but my favorite mascara comes from BeautiControl. I fell in love with the products years ago, and what Melaleuca does not have, BeautiControl does. I swear that I am just falling apart, but from Saudi, I picked up this weird rash that comes out all over, and most products from the stores completely irritate my skin.

I like candles, but there are many with dyes and other substances in them which bother me. One of my friends was selling them, JewelScent I enjoyed them a lot, but I have so many other mini-businesses. I decided to teach my daughter who is in college, about entrepreneurship, (who will graduate this June, YEA!). I gave her a spot that clicks from my main site too. The candles have rings inside them, a surprise, like cracker jacks! They also have the aroma beads, which I use some of them with the Battle Buddies. At the same time, teaching my daughter about business, I am also teaching her to pay it forward. A percentage of all the sales goes to women veterans and their families.

Wow, I feel like a commercial. I have listed them here for two purposes. The first using the funds to help out other women veterans and MST survivors. But also because many of us are disabled and cannot have a normal 9 to 5 job. Or, for me, any job that relies on me being there at certain times. It just does not work so well when you come in the morning and before everyone else has settled in, you have to go because of a migraine. Or, which happens a lot, I am no longer a people person. I used to be, the social butterfly, prior to the military and a little into it, but after it, no. I keep to myself most days. I am not isolating myself. I am taking care of myself, and that sometimes demands not being around a lot of people.

It is very difficult to feel productive when you do not know if the next hour you will be functionable, or not. I thought that helping veterans, face to face, would be okay. It would have been, but just as others have found out, the evilness of people is relentless. I questioned if I should mention my disabilities, and thought because it was a veteran's program and a mental health organization, it would be fine. It was not. I tried it, and it just did not turn out to be what I want to do. I love making the Battle Buddies. I enjoy having people ask about my MST charms and I can educate them. I am fond of introducing people to some great companies, and I appreciate being able to go online and have the privilege of meeting other women veterans, who experienced MST. I adore writing, and hope that I can continue to do so (troubles from the TBI is making it a little more problematic these days).

There are business you can do from home that can be very fulfilling. It also keeps me attached to the world. I tend to back off and stop interacting with people, so having the businesses, I keep myself out there. I cannot do the volunteering, so this is one of the ways I can pay it forward. I assistance others with their businesses, and make sure they understand paying it forward.

Why all this business stuff? Along with what I mentioned before, a good foundation for a purposeful life is self-reliance. This world isn't getting any better, and being self-reliant gives a sense of security. It does not just include the ability to pay your bills, but also to be able to give back to society. Many people volunteer, but some of us have a hard time finding a fit with everything else we have going on. I would love to go back and help other women veterans out, face-to-face, but to be able to help out another successfully, you have to take care of yourself first. With all my issues of smells, lights, people, there are still things that I can do, and I do them. But to be able to do them, I must have my own house in order. Being self-reliant also encompasses being prepared for emergencies. Oh there are many that nobody can be prepared for, but there is so much that we can do ourselves, to make sure if a natural disaster does happen, you already have a plan, and that is a huge help during the storm. Having drinkable water, food, an ability to cook, flashlights, lanterns, and more. We have a 48 hour kit. In it is enough to sustain us for 48 hours. It also includes a medical kit, and medications. I have been taught this from a small child, at church. And I have used it on occasion, having lived in California and Texas. There have been storms in Texas where our electricity went out for four days. Our whole neighborhood was black, except for our house. My family was fine. We had everything that we needed, and knew how to use it, and by doing that we were able to help others. Other times it has been the finances that have been the emergency. It has been a blessing to have the emergency money, because of car issues, microwave died, washer decided it was done, and other glitches you just do not think are going to happen.

I came around the road and looked over to my house. There were flames over the back of the house. My whole back yard was on fire. We lived in east Texas and our back yard was acres of trees and shrubs. I had my son with me. So as I called 911, then my husband, I was getting the hose on one side and my son was on the other side of the house. Our hold out was to keep the fire from getting to any of the buildings, which contained gas, oil, and so many other combustible products. Had we not known how to battle a fire, the both of us, we would have lost the house and everything in it. We were blessed and kept the fire away from the buildings until the volunteer fire fighters got there. I thought about what would have happened had it all went up in flames, and I was comforted to know that it would not ruin us. Sure it would be horrible, and there would be a lot lost, but we were prepared. We had our vital documents in the fire proof safe. In the other fire proof save we had back up cash, and other stuff. We would have been fine. But it was that and other natural disasters, we have been through, which I am thankful I was taught self-reliance as well as preparedness, all from church.

Being self-reliant gives me the extra time to be able to help others, and extra funds to not cause worry in the house, helping others. That is one of the many reasons why I have businesses, teach others about having their own, as well as being in the service to others. A purposeful life is not just thinking about yourself, but what you can do for others. Because as the scriptures say, when you are in the service of others, you are in the service of your God.

What would you like to do to help others? What will it take to get there? How self-reliant are you? How prepared are you for emergencies?

And the King shall answer and say
unto them, Verily I say unto you,
Inasmuch as ye have done in unto one of
the least of these my brethren, ye have
done it unto me. – Matt. 25:40

Relationships

The majority of family and friends will not understand what you have been through. They might feel they somehow could not protect you. You wondered why you did or did not do what they think you should have done. Sexual assaults have always been seen as shameful, that somehow the person has been damaged. They are not of the same value anymore. This is a seriously destructive myth.

Every person no matter what they have done or what has been done to them, has divine worth. Having negative people around you will drag you lower than you are now. Do not think that I am saying you should put on a pair of rose colored glasses and skip down the road pretending all is good.

Have you ever had a friend or relative that every time you are with them, you just do not have a good time? Afterwards you always feel upset or angry? These are toxic relationships. You should try to surround yourself with positive, supportive people. I have a friend who called her mom when she was having problems, just to hear over and over how much of a screw-up she was. That all the choices she made (which ended negatively) were her fault and stupid. Finally, after listening to her a few times I asked the question, "Why call? You know what she will say. Why do that to yourself?" She gave the answer many would, "It's my mother." I am not a respecter of blood relatives. There is no person who has the right, relative or not, to verbally abuse you. Verbal abuse does not only include being called names but also accusing you of any responsibility for the assault.

Along with verbal abuse there is no person who has a right to physically abuse you. At times, we have confused thoughts that we are with the abusive person because that is all that we are worth. No one else will ever love us and so we stay with an abuser. I am here to tell you there are millions of men and women who do not verbally or physically abuse their girl/boyfriend, fiancé or spouse. With the Internet and matching sites, you have the ability to find one of those million who would love to be in a relationship with you. If intimacy and trust of that nature, you cannot cope with, at this time, then a friendship site. If you want to have a bunch of friends there are literally millions of people out there who have experienced sexual trauma(s) and there are hundreds of thousands who have experienced MST, that are looking for friendship-level intimacy. So seek them out.

Set boundaries that you feel comfortable with and do not apologize for them. Many times after an assault, our boundary/limits are all jumbled. We feel that we are being overly cautious, so we allow others into our personal space that we would not have before. In your mind, you could think "What signal was I giving off that caused the assault?" or "If I said no and no didn't mean no then how do I really say no?" Sometimes all physical contact feels dirty. You know the person loves you and you want them to hug or kiss you, but when it all feels the same, how can you discern when it is too far or too fast? You argue with yourself that you are being weird or odd and that this is a common thing in a relationship, but your body screams yuck. It will take time and others who truly are supportive to understand. When it begins to feel dirty, do not just continue because you have rationalized to yourself that it is a normal part of a relationship. That somehow you need to get over it; that is totally false. As well as setting physical boundaries, set emotional ones too. It is vital to give yourself the time to reconstruct and identify with the "now you."

Emotional Vampires

Have you ever known someone who after you're finished visiting you are emotionally exhausted? These are people I like to call emotional vampires. They feed off all your emotions. The emotions you have after hearing all about their struggles. It is completely a one-way relationship, helping themselves out and leaving you depleted. You probably were the one who called and asked to get together because you had a really bad day. A few sentences into what happened and the conversation has completely changed, once again, to her. No matter how things start, you always end up helping her out with her problems, listening to her vent, wondering if there is ever going to be your turn. She always pleads for advice, help, something from you. I've had a few people I knew fall into this classification, and I quickly distanced myself from them.

Having just one emotional vampire is exhaustive, but more than one and that's all you'll ever have time for. It adds to what is already draining on your system. Emotional Vampires flock to people who have good hearts and want to help. Sometimes we forget that there is a give and take to healthy relationships. Vampires are not healthy, they only take.

Conflict cannot survive without your participation. – Wayne Dyer

---

Self-Care
When recovering from any ailment, taking extra care of the self is essential. Many of these recommendations will not be easy to make into habits. However, all are to better our health, allowing the most optimal environment, to assist in the healing process. Consulting all health care providers is necessary before implementing any new life-style change, along with doing ample amounts of research.

'You are what you eat.' Nobody likes the word diet, it has a negative connotation and gives the impression of doing without, being restricted, and limiting the nummy stuff. Diet usually is seen as limited to just food and drink, but I am talking about much more than that. I am talking about addressing a positive life-style change, looking at the whole you, your whole environment. It places more of a focus on the cornucopia of possibilities than concentrating over the deficiencies, and most of these deficiencies are harmful anyway. Before beginning any changes see a doctor and if the VA clinic has a dietitian, then get an appointment and convey you would like to make your life healthier.

In the beginning, it is advantageous for you to keep a daily Healthy Log, or Journal. This healthy log is to record all the items which are being worked on. Within the health journal, or as a separate journal, is the Food Log; listing the foods and drinks that are taken into the body, notating the amount and time of the day. Sometimes it is shocking to realize how much is put into the body without truly comprehending the food, how much is eaten, and at what times. Now, do not be discouraged if your VA Dietitian turns out like mine did, an overweight, chain-smoking, uninformed person who only printed off the official government "food plate." She asked if I was on ebenefits and healthevet. That I could find a bunch of information about how to stay healthy there. I was looking for much more than giving me some sites to try and find my own answers. I wanted specific answers about my health, with my issues, and the effects with my medications.

Look over the food packages you purchase and try purchasing the ones with lower sugar, lower salt, less dyes and less processed foods. I heard that you should not eat anything with ingredients you cannot pronounce. If I tried that I would die of starvation. Okay I wouldn't but sometimes yellow dye #5 tastes really good. Looking up some questionable ingredients on the internet or inquiring about them from your nutritionist, is a good idea. I noticed I was having more headaches and migraines. I had added gum back into my life. That's when I learned most all gum now contains aspertaine, a known migraine trigger. There are very few which actually have fructose corn syrup, let alone actual sugar.

The items to exclude all together: alcohol, coffee, tea (non-herbal), energy drinks, any type of tobacco products, and any illegal drugs. I would be very careful in self medicating. Illegal drugs are not the only worry. You can get prescription medication from the VA that zombieizes you. There is no reason to be so medicated that you can only sit on the couch and stare at the TV. It's unfortunate and I've been there, so drugged that I was completely unfunctionable. It was not living. Sure I did not have any emotional problems, I had no problems. I also had no emotions, no joy, no love, no real thoughts, a zombie, and not the fast moving type. There are going to be some who completely disagree with some of these recommendations. Especially the ones to eliminate; however, this is the best optimal start for the healing process.

When excluding caffeine, I mean to exclude it in high doses, I always hear, "well chocolate has caffeine in it so my coffee and soda is fine." Not necessarily. It would take about 30 normal regular size candy bars to equal one cup of roasted brewed coffee (and there are other noxious ingredients in coffee. That is why it is on the exclude list). There are so many sodas which add caffeine to them, it is not for flavor but to get you addicted and medicated. Sodas also add high amounts of sugar, much more than your body should have on any day. I like sodas too, so I limit myself to them; they are treats, not something to grab when I am thirsty.

Now the haves. You should begin to eat a lot more variety of vegetables. (Side note: Chocolate comes from a bean. Beans are vegetables; therefore, chocolate is a vegetable. Yep, still in denial on some things.) Increase your intake of fresh fruits and plenty of water. As one Jimmy Newtron villain called humans "water sacks;" it is actually an extremely important consideration. My dog has allergy issues. We had been told by the vet it was probably seasonal, caused by grasses and weeds. Then I moved and within a week she looked like she was on her death bed. Hair was coming out, red marks and sores all over and lethargic. We tried all different foods, thinking it had to be that since there were not enough weeds or grasses to cause the allergies (she is mostly an inside dog). The only difference we could tell was the water. It only took three days and she went from death bed to completely annoying, wanting her ball tossed all the time – normal. We bought a water filer which came with one of those testers and sure enough our city water was (in mine and others' opinions) toxic. It smelled like chlorine and had a metallic after taste to it. Test your water and see if it is contaminated, and do not rely on what the government thinks is okay. Their opinion of toxic is not the same as the opinion that my body has, or my dog's. What's in your water?

Organic foods are most desirable, ones with the least amount of pesticides, processing and human manipulation. Just going into the local market and stocking up on their fruits and vegetables is not enough. Unfortunately, the produce in most local grocery stores has been in some way manufactured. Human-engineered produce, the manipulation of genes for pest protection and other reasons, is not natural. Just as what happens in the majority part of the meat and dairy industry, with its processes. I remember as a child going onto the front porch and picking up the glass jars of milk after the milkman delivered them. Milk was delivery at least twice a week, because fresh milk sours that quickly. There is nothing natural about milk and bread sitting on store shelves for weeks and still being consumable.

Meat should be eaten sparingly, and not at every meal. You can get protein from a variety of other foods than just meats. For milk, cheese and egg products, you should discuss them with your dietitian. Many victims have complaints about gastrointestinal problems, so go slow to figure out which foods will cause discomfort. Still keep in mind you should take all GOOD things slowly and in moderation. Not like some say "All things in moderation." Or even "All natural things in moderation." Hemlock is natural, in moderation – you're dead. Your body requires the time to adjust to the new routine, do not try to jump in with everything all at once. It can be that simple.

It is not optimal for fruits and vegetables to ripen on trucks. Putting additives into foods, to allow the shelf life to increase, does not increase the nutrients of the product; but in fact decreases it. The best possible foods are the most natural foods, in their natural state (the non-poisonous and non-toxic ones). I have found a company I really like- *Thrive Life*, which has freeze-dried food. I love being able to make meals that are more robust for me than the products at the local grocery store. I also don't throw away food like I used to. I use what I need. Click to my main web site (Justcrafty.com) if you are interested in making easier and healthier meals, especially if you do not have access to a farmers market. (And again all the revenues will go to help women veterans and MST survivors).

I have found that eating small amounts of food more than the average three meals a day helps me not feel the hunger to want to gorge myself. And that my blood sugar is kept at a constant level. Understand, I am not the perfection of health, and there are times when I stumble back into old habits. What has kept me going is that my blueprint is not some dietitian's dream; it is a realistic plan for my life. I do not beat myself up over slips; I am human.

When you are treating yourself because of an accomplishment, try not to have it be any type of food or drink. Find other ways to celebrate, like taking a longer walk, watching a great movie more than once, allowing yourself to stay in on a Saturday reading a book. When we are in the habit of treating ourselves with food, we can associate that accomplished enjoyment with the good tastes and feeling of being 'fed' (nourished). It can cause an automatic reach to food every time we want to feel good. Pavlov's dogs did not get the food all the time after it had been associated with the bell. The bell just had to be rung for them to start to salivate.

Around You

Trying to determine the optimal environment is extremely challenging because we are all so very dissimilar in this area, but here are some points to think about. Look around your home and take inventory of all the possessions you have. Many of us have so much stuff packed all around that it can even be hard to freely walk around the house. De-cluttering and prioritizing will take a while, but if you can do a small amount every day, you will be surprised at how quickly this can be done. I have started so many projects, but there is not enough time in three lifetimes to be able to get to them all. I have had to pigeonhole everything, placing the most important projects on top. This list, however, is not written in stone. It should be a continually reevaluated list, projects move up and down, off and on.

I have difficulty with getting rid of items. What if I needed that? It is not junk so why depart with it? One of my control issues has been to want to keep everything, assuming that someday I may require it. If I don't have it, then I was not prepared, and I should be prepared. This stems from my maladjusted thoughts of "not being prepared" to be attacked. It has been hard, and still is. However, when whatchamacallits are not cluttering my space, there is more room for my mind to breathe. Inventory it all: clothes, shoes, purses, belts, books, photos, knickknacks, jewelry (I must admit I like pretty shinny things), everything. You are beginning to get it. You should evaluate how often you use the item, and what emotional value you have attached to it (and that can be a session all its own with your therapist). If it is easier to just go out and buy it or do you really have to have it taking up precious space in the first place? Choosing what to keep and what not to, can be emotionally draining and if you desire some third-party input ask a close friend. But do not allow that friend to have the ultimate say so, if something stays or goes, just where on the list they see the item as it applies to you.

Pretty Picture

What are on the walls in your home? What do you see every time you walk into the room? Pictures you have up can affect your mood. My walls were eclectic (I'm in the process of moving), if viewing them as whole. I had a huge still life painting of flowers, fruits, and vases with an elaborate golden colored wooden frame hanging on the wall, where I would eat and usually do my work at. I loved the rich colors, they calm me, but I also like the fresh fruit; it prompted better choices. A number of times I had been working and felt the urge to snack, looked up at the picture and went and got an apple instead of thinking about it. More than likely I would have had something sweet and not so healthy for me, without that visual suggestion.

Down the hallway was the ordinary cascade of family photos, my family. Now hold that thought. I did not have pictures of my childhood family, and it was purposeful. That childhood family was abusive when I was a child and not supportive when I told them after the assaults; so they were not on the walls. It is not disrespecting them, it is respecting me. When I looked at the walls, and even if I have had a fight with my children or husband, the photos are of the whimsical, joyful, frolicsome times. Even if upset, it was hard not to smile when I saw them and that is why they were there. I had a picture of the temple I was married in and other religious pictures, all which brought happy, comforting, smiling, calming, spiritual thoughts and feelings to me without consciously thinking about them. That is what you hunger for, positive and uplifting reminders on all the walls. This is not a green light for making scrapbook walls. There should to be blank spaces between them. Enough so that when you look at the wall, the pictures are instantly the focal point. No need for scanning to separate them.

Paint by Numbers

Many people do not realize the emotional responses that are automatic when you see different colors. Just as critical as what is on the wall is the color of that wall. Sit down and look at just colors. There are books which list what the common emotional response is for that color, to the general population. We all have our favorites and ones that we cannot explain, but just annoy the heck out of us. Luckily, both my husband and I agree we do not like the color yellow. As an accent color it is fine, like a lemon in a picture. But even on a small portion of a wall, that color would drive both him and me nuts, wanting to take a hammer to it. I feel the calmest with warm tans, browns and greens. In rooms that I mostly work, I like it a little more vibrant. It gets the creative mind going, still no yellow. If you happen to be renting and not allowed to change the color of the walls, you can purchase large pieces of material and put them up. There are a number of materials out there able to be used without damaging the walls. It sounds extreme, but as I said most do not realize colors can have the ability to evoke emotions without our conscious knowledge. In this respect, white and black are not the absence of color – white, and all colors – black, but an emotional white and emotional black.

Flowers

Smell your rooms. What does each room smell like? There are certain scents which also give common responses. Consider the function of the room and what smell should enhance it. Yes this does sound a little silly, but did you know that olfactory stimulations are the only ones that goe directly to the brain? All others, touch, taste, sight and hearing go through a manager, for the simplest of analogies. This does not imply that all through your house, when you step into each room, you are bombarded with roses here and vanilla there. They should be subtle, and each room does not have to be different. Just as color is not given much credit, smells are not either, and both make such a difference. Again just as with colors there are scents which do not follow the common pattern.

Most people like lavender to calm them down, using it in a bath or in the bedroom. I cannot stand the smell anywhere around me. My reaction is to get away from it, and if I have to stay, it aggravates me. There may be scents and color triggers for you and even after years and years they still can bring up negative emotions. So before you light another scented candle and wonder why you are not getting the rest or rejuvenation from it. Think back, is it a trigger? You do not have to know the exact reasons certain colors or smells upset you to not have them in your home. I do not know why I hate the color yellow or the smell of lavender, but it is not essential to know to keep them out of my life. A cautious note with scents, spraying chemicals into the air, such as air fresheners, is not good for your health. Many air fresheners only deaden your ability to smell, not take the odor out. Fresh flowers, open windows, essential oils, and some natural candles are much better than the unreadable list of chemicals found in most air sprays. I like the smell of the JewelScent candles, they use natural materials. They also have scented aroma beads, soaps, scrubs, and more.

Chemicals

One of my husband's annoying sayings over the years has been, "dirt doesn't hurt." I have now found some wisdom in that statement. Not that a dirty house is a healthy house, but a super clean house can be just as (or even more) harmful. Pull out all the chemicals you use for cleaning and start to read the labels. You should try and find products which are not as corrosive and harmful. For centuries people have cleaned their houses without the array of harsh products we use today. Since we've added them, it would seem this would indicate fewer diseases. Yet it appears there are more sick people today than in the past. Over the years we have been slowly poisoning ourselves and negatively affecting our passed-on dna. Yet it seems most people do not see this connection. Try to take account for everything that goes into your body, on your body, and that is around your body. To become more educated to what is harming your body. Because of my time in Saudi Arabia, and exposure to invasive chemicals, I know am very sensitive to smells as well as chemicals. For cleaning I use Melaleuca an ecofriendly company reduces waste, and they have the same attitude, harsh chemicals should not be around us.

The lighting of a room can also affect the reactions you are having in that room. Real sun light is the best. There should be ample light in all the rooms. Even if you do not use that room all the time, as in the bedroom. This can be incredibly difficult when you live close to others and opening your curtains allows them visual access to your space. It can feel like another violation. You do crave light, sun light, so if at all possible go outside, go somewhere safe, with someone safe and be out in the sun. This also is difficult when winter weather does not allow the sun to come out, still try to get to where there is actual natural light. One of the theories for the term "winter depression" is that it is caused by the shortened days of sunlight accompanied with most people being inside working during that time. How often do you go to and from work in the dark? Are you inside all day long with fluorescents glaring down on you? I am very sensitive to lights, especially florescent. Can't stand them; they cause migraines. So at times, I wear sunglasses inside. Mostly at appointments which always seem to have the annoying florescent, especially at the VA. During your breaks or lunch time try to get to the sun.

Ask, and it shall be given you; seek, and ye shall find; knock, and it shall be opened unto you: - Matt 7:7

Exercise

I am not a happy camper in this department. At times, I have tallied getting up out of bed, walking into the kitchen, lifting the one gallon container of milk and then walking into the living room, as a part of my daily listed "exercise." If you see me running down the street, you should run. There is either a fire or someone after me, because I am not doing it without serious cause. I applaud anyone who can get up and run a bunch of miles before breakfast, but do not think that I am the least bit envious. I know, I also have heard that people who run live longer, but that longer living time is spent running, so I'll pass.

A growing health predicament is the over consumption of food that has countless atrocious ingredients in it, the pounds slowly escalate. I used to be that person, who was envied, I could eat all I wanted and never gain a pound. In the military, it was forced PT, time taken to exercise. Unfortunately, not having that forced time anymore and the added on injuries, and age, it has given away to not a lot of physical exercise. I do like to walk, not speed walk, or competition walk, no dog dragging walk, but just a nice pace. I like to lift weights when I am watching TV, but remember it is not power-lifting for me. What I am trying to get at is if you do not like to do it at all; whether it is running, aerobics, competition walking, etc. Adding a huge amount of it to a plan to get healthier is not going to work. Find something you like to do, but do something. Move during the day, get out of your seat, off the couch, out of the car; whatever it is and make that blood work for a living. Make sure to speak with your doctor before trying to incorporate any new exercise program into your life.

After getting hurt, not only did I just not like to have some gym-type exercise, it hurt, really hurt. Then kids came along but what tipped me over the edge of the scale, was the negative weight-gaining side-effect of my medications. Many anti-depressants and other medications used to treat symptoms of PTSD, along with the other military-caused medical issues I have, cause weight-losing complications. Not only the weight but when depression sets in, the small want to keep in shape heads out the window. So I have to scrutinize what I'm taking in, the medication-induced cravings, medication-induced fatigue, mental illness symptoms of depression; it all adds up. It has been a struggle sometimes, but I continually tell myself that I am doing the best I can. I have multiple different pant sizes to tolerate the weight changes. I have a parameter I've set. One thought-through, incorporating all my medical issues, age, and medication that I am happy with it. I will never be the size I used to be. I am not that person anymore, and it would be unrealistic and obsessive to try.

True enjoyment comes from activity of the mind and exercise of the body; the two are ever united. – Humboldt

---

Journaling

Journaling has been around for thousands of years but the therapeutic benefits of it usually are not thought about. When talking about journaling most people think of a teenager girl on her bed writing with some pink fuzzy pen about boys, but the benefits of what seems a childish dribble onto pages, is so much more. Writing can be very freeing. When you write your thoughts and feelings down, then read them back, you could uncover something you never thought about or connected before.

I have been an avid journal writer from age thirteen. I literally have boxes full of journals which pretty much chronologically lay out my entire life's story. I also seemed to have the same type of communication with my journal as in some novels. I did not name it, but I had the unconscious impression that I always had somewhere to unleash my feelings. There was no judgement as I wrote. I did not try and fix the issue. Sometimes it was just writing and my journal was listening intently to everything I wrote, that helped.

So where do you start? Heading out to the local office supply store and picking up some generic notebook has never been my style, other researchers seem to agree. These are your personal thoughts and should be enclosed in something more respectable than what you would use for a grocery list. I have trolled the web and found unique journals from reasonable to outrageous in price. I have even made my own. It's a personal thing, like a purse, something that fits your style, at that stage in your life.

Most people who are hesitant about journaling state they do not know what to say. That blank paper seems to be intimidating. First, forget proper English (I did writing this book). This is not a paper you are handing in for a grade. In fact nobody has to ever see what you write. It is not necessary to spell correctly, or use proper grammar – write how you speak. Try not to sensor yourself. If you want to doodle or draw, this is your journal. I still write with pen and paper, in an actual book. There have been studies that state the connection between moving your hands to the letters, instead of pushing a button, seems to be significantly much more beneficial. One added benefit is the ability to permanently 'delete' your entries. Although many say that you can do that on a computer, since most all computers also use the internet, the ability for more than just your personal information to be hijacked is there. There are many people who have mistakenly sent off the wrong files in emails enough times that I do not chance it.

I have noticed by not just dating my entries, but giving the time of day and where I am writing at, helps bring a deeper understanding to what I wrote. Looking back at different times of the day the entry was written, opens a whole new insight I might have missed had I just dated it. It might seem redundant but I also include the day of the week. Example – "Monday......4:30 pm....07 Sept 15, (office desk). I have at times gone back a few days and figured out it really was not that date. I am much better with the days of the week now, and fine with crossing out the incorrect ones.

A happy journal, or log, whichever you feel more comfortable with, is where you can write down the good days, the accomplishments, the funny stories and everything positive. It can be in great detail or just a few sentences. But all the things which are in it are positive. This is in addition to your regular journal, when the other days come, pull it out and read. When you feel like nothing is going right, pick up the journal and read. When you are feeling overwhelmed, again, pick it up and read. You'll be amazed at all the things you forget that are blessings in your life, that you've accomplished and good days, that seemed to have slipped away.

The nicest part is being able to write down all my thoughts and feelings; otherwise, I might suffocate. – Anne Frank

---

Medications

Like everything else, this is a very personal decision. The decision to take or not take medications, which ones and for how long is individual. Medications are not an end all to eliminating the symptoms. They help relieve or reduce some of them while you are working through the underlined problems. Medications alone just masks some of the symptoms. That is the issue, it is recommended to be doing some type of therapy with medications, taking them alone will just continue the symptoms, which will continue the need to take them for the rest of your life. And can lead to their abuse. Most cocktail of medications, which suppress symptoms from experiencing trauma, do not necessarily lead to a successful functional life, especially when prescribed by the VA.

I do not rely on anyone else to decide what medications and how much to take. I use the information from my psychiatrist as a suggestion. In the past, I have allowed the VA to give me what they determined was vital and ended up sitting on my couch drooling. I was zombified. When it was mentioned to the VA doctors that I couldn't function on a basic level; there did not seem to be a problem with it. I did not have any of the symptoms anymore. So, they asked what was the dilemma? The VA was right; I did not have any symptoms. I also didn't have any feelings. That was the problem. I wanted to still be a part of this world. I had a husband and children and wanted to have emotions, feel something, anything.

I have the horror stories of the VA and dispensing medications, where if I had taken the ones prescribed by different doctors, who did not seem to want to look in my file to know what I was taking, I would have died. Another time, when I was pregnant, I was prescribed a medication with sever birth-defects without any warnings. Didn't take that either. My medical charts are riddled with doctor notes about side-effects, and how we talked about the medications before being prescribed. They were in the notes but it never happened. Now I have no problems questioning the doctors about the medications that they think I should take. It is my life and I have the right to decide.

There are many questions when taking medications – what are the potential side-effects? Is it addictive? Has there been long-term studies? How much will I have to take? How often during the day?

Is there things I cannot eat or drink while on them? Can I take them and be pregnant? Will they interact with what I'm already on? If yes, how? These are not all the possible questions to ask, just a few examples. There are many medications that can be used for a multiple of symptoms that you could be suffering from. So questioning the doctor/psychiatrist about the possibility of another medication being used, is not only perfectly fine, but necessary. Especially when you are considering if it has side-effects that you are not willing to trade off for the reduction of specific symptoms. That seems to be one of the major problems with medications, sometimes the side-effects are worse than the symptoms they are supposed to be helping with. I think I have been through the alphabet of medications and there are some that seem to work better, but the trade-offs of the side-effects were not at all worth it. I teetered between reducing the symptoms and feeling drugged. And I will not take the ones which cause: too light-headedness, shaky, headaches, feeling like I have to throw up, confused, out of touch with reality, migraines and more, I have a list and I want to function.

I also do my own research and yes, it is online, but I use sites that are reputable and if there is a question, I wait to see the doctor again. And yes, some do become quite irritated at it. But this is my right as a patient. It is also very entertaining when you say, "I'd like a second opinion." VA doctors do not seem to hear that often enough.

It was the normal appointment. I had already been seen for years there, this was just a medication refill when I hit an obstacle. The mental health personnel, who I'd seen once before, began the checklist of questions as if this was my first appointment. Sure enough the question came about experiencing any unwanted sexual contact in the military. I have been told that the question is only asked once, then it just appears on your charts. I get it asked all the time. I really wish it would stop. Why ask over and over and over when I have already answered yes? I rolled my eyes just wondering if she'd actually read at least the summary of my file, or her own notes from the last appointment I had with her.

The questions continued and it got to the "Are your meds working." My reply is always the truth and usually same, "They work well enough." Again, off into the reasons as to why they just work well enough. I explained it all over and at the end it comes down to taking just enough to stay functional. I do not want the outrageous chemicals that play out in my head when I'm on nothing; but I also do not want to be numb or in a vegetative state of couch potato.

She questioned about my sleep. How can I really function well without good rest? I explain I usually get the minimum to stay functional. I cannot have a normal job with specific hours or days, but I can be tired around the house. Yes, the sleeping pills give me more sleep time, but they also cause more vivid dreams. I suffer from nightmares, more vivid dreams can morph into more vivid nightmares. So I limit myself to taking them only when necessary. If I need to get up early in the morning, for some appointment, or if I would not be able to get any sleep without them; that is when I take them.

But don't I want to sleep? Sure, but it is at a price. The drug-fog the next day, the increased headaches and vivid dreams are a trade-off for getting sleep. She did not like my explanation. She questioned if I have ever tried this drug or that one. I have tried so many, why the VA does not just create a spread sheet of all the meds and the reasons they did not work is beyond me. (Well not really, it would be helpful that's why there isn't one.) Sure I could, but then every time we'd have to go through 50 or so meds. Then the offers of new medications are truly that, new. Not something that I tried years ago. Since I'm not currently taking it, there was a severe reactional reasoning, but I haven't got the vaguest idea what it was. I can barely remember the active medications I take now, let alone what I tried 10, even 20 years ago for a few weeks. I am pretty much tired of being somebodies guinea pig. Changing medications is not like changing your clothes or even your eating habits. It is a process, one that removes me from most obligations and can increase other medical issues I suffer from. You have a right to fully participate in decisions about medications. And (unless hospitalized) have a right to refuse them too. Have you ever been bullied or talked into taking them? What happened?

I became frustrated at the continual insistence of her trying to change what was working for my functioning level. My psychiatrist, her supervisor, has discussed all of that with me months ago. The psychiatrist was okay with my decisions but who I was seeing wasn't. She became irritated. I did not just accept she "knew" if I just tired it, it would be better. The ultimate came as she took this printed message off her wall and placed it before me. The quote was in effect taking responsibility for my own treatment. She accused me of not trying, just giving up. She then became cynical, if she got me an appointment with someone else, it would not matter, would it? That I was not trying to help myself, as if I had fallen into the helplessness victim arena. Her statement was directed to the symptoms of PTSD, and she spoke like I wanted to continue to have these problems. She was right, it didn't matter if I got another appointment with anyone, I wasn't budging.

Had she actually looked into my records beyond the diagnosis of PTSD to see that many of the symptoms could be attributed to something else, she might not have discounted them. I am not PTSD, and for this VA mental health "professional" to treat me as a single diagnosis, not a person, infuriated me. As if I had no other medical problems. My verbiage, posture and tone changed, that was it; I was finished. My only reason now for this appointment was to make her re-prescribe another three months of medications. The ones I was already on. I could tell she was not about to just refill my prescriptions, whether I wanted to or not. She essentiality was saying I HAD to try the medications she had "suggested."

I wanted to yell, "Look, just give me my meds!" And then realized the irony of it. I had gotten to this point, not because I did not want to get better, to try something else, or to take responsibility for my own healing. No, it was because of the high and mighty, 'self-knowing,' VA mental health "professional" thought she knew better than I did. It was now a battle, that she was ill prepared for. I have had to utilize the VA system for over 20 years and have been through a lot of garbage. I was not about to let someone who only scanned, (if at all) my medical files decide what I did and did not need to take. Eventually, she gave up trying to change my mind. She was not happy about it and her treatment to me reflected that.

As I left the room, with my medications refilled, I thought about how this would have played out differently had I not understood the VA system and been younger and more naïve. She did not ask why I didn't want to change them, just assumed it was lack of determination. She wasn't interested in discussing any alternative. Especially with what I would and would not trade off, for side-effects. If it would help, or cause months of mental and physical torture until I got back on that schedule, she did not care. What I did know, was that any change would cause physical pain of some level, and more than likely a type of emotional roller coaster. How high and low I'd get was just as unknowing as riding a rollercoaster for the first time without seeing it.

A strong positive attitude will create more miracles than any wonder drug. – Patricia Neal

---

72

5

TRUST & BETRYAL

The Blame Game

So why is it, that in sexual assault/harassment incidents, the victim is the one who is blamed? Is the person who is burglarized blamed for having a house? Is the mugged person blamed for having money? No. So again why does it seem to change when it is sexual assault?

The media has portrayed acts of violence and intimacy occurring simultaneously so often it can be viewed as a normal occurrence. Too many times the media depicts if a woman says no she really does not mean that. She is saying that you are not aggressively persuasive enough for it to change into a yes. This is reinforced by telling girls when they are hurt (physically or verbally) by boys, that he just likes you. What you are essentially condoning is the further victimization of girls and subsequently women, telling them that violence is a part of love. The assailant uses the blame game to divert their responsibility and actions, for their choice to attack, by rationalizing there was something the victim did, which provoked or made them attack. The myths assailants use to justify their choices are just as variant.

First off, nobody deserves to be sexually assaulted, no matter what their character is, or what they have done. I completely disagree with sexually assaulting rapists as punishment; death is better. Not vigilante death, but through the laws and courts, the death penalty should be able to be put on the table in most cases. Especially in the cases where children were the victims. In the military, the minimum of a conviction for attempted sexual assault, should be: time in prison, a dishonorable discharge and must register as a sex offender for the rest of their lives. That is for an attempt, but just as with civilians, the death penalty should be on the table for most military convictions of sexual assault. If someone feels this is too punitive, guess what? The perpetrator chose it.

To make sure the delusion of this 'safe fantasy world' exists, a person must assign a false perception of victim-control to all situations. The assumption is that if you can pinpoint these 'so-called' manageable reasons and if you do not do them, you will not be victimized. One such 'controllable reason' would be that the survivor is a bad person; consequently, "bad things happen to bad people." Another is the victim made a wanton and or dangerous choice; therefore if I know what that choice was and do not do it, I will not be assaulted. This secures the fantasy of safety and the illusion of a just world theory.

Unfortunately, there are many who try to argue assumed reasons for the assault by attributing them to your actions. We make thousands of choices every day, some are considered good; others can be neutral or bad. Sometimes the only reason a choice is placed into the bad column is because of the outcome. Other choices, such as drinking and getting into a car, can be seen as bad to some from the beginning, without the conclusion of an assault. Everyone is allowed to make bad choices, but that does not suggest anyone has a right to assault another person. Making yourself vulnerable is not a "green light" to being assaulted. There is only one choice that makes any difference and that one choice was the perpetrator choosing to attack. There is no shame or guilt involved with being a victim, that should, but more than likely does not, fall entirely on the perpetrator.

Survivors can be bamboozled into this misguided ideology and self-blame, especially when evil or uninformed persons show studies statistically giving percentages to specific factors, called risk factors. It does not matter what any study or theory toward sexual assault/harassment claims to reveal, as risk factors. The fact remains, no victim is to blame for the assault, not a single bit! Luckily nowadays most studies recognize this and are using the data collected for other reasons (i.e. more police patrols in certain areas, start community-based programs, educating the public). All of this is great; however, most completely miss the reason behind the assaults. The focus is on the risk factors, which are usually victim-centered, or conditions of the physical environment and the military has joined in with this idea. I do understand educating about risk factors, adding police patrols in high-risk areas, and starting programs. But even more than pointing out those victim-centered risk factor; how about we education about the perp's risk factors? Educating our boys to become men, not thugs. And it does start at home. It dawns by taking the responsibility to make sure you are not a part of the problem; actually creating, encouraging, and composing, these thugs.

Most programs that I have seen in the military, targeted towards active duty are victim-centered, -"What can you do so that you are not a victim?" From the buddy system to talking about sa/sh, all centered on the actions of the victim. Other parts, just as in civilian programs, focalize on the physical environmental risks. At the same time it is a bottoms up philosophy. Talking to women service members, it is imperative to be a top-down focus instead.

Factors of a Sexual Perpetrator
I would love to be able to bullet point the characteristics of these jerks. However, that is what allows them to hide out in plain sight, mixed in with the population, any population and even any sub-population. I pulled up study after study, and there were some correlations, but most reflected the environment more than actual character traits, and/or easily observable behaviors. The studies themselves had so many unknown variables that my attempts made

me feel as though I was trying to figure out a complicated math problem that the experts cannot. The largest of the found studies focused on mainly two groups – convicted criminals and college students, and neither group is comparable to the military. I read studies which indicated most sexual offenders had been victimized as children. I read others which called this childhood victimization a myth, that most were not victims. Each new study took off the list a trait, added to the list, or both. Risk factors which were numbered more times than excluded were:

- Pornography use.
- Impulsive tendencies.
- Anti-Social behaviors.
- Dominant.
- Aggressive.
- Expert in rationalizing their actions.

Environmental Risk Factors for Military

Branch. There is a different level of risk to each branch; however, most studies indicate the Army has the highest risk; then Navy, Marine Corps, and last Air Force. It was continually noted, that the three, Army, Navy and Marine Corps change in position on some studies but the Air Force not only repeatedly has the lowest risk, but by such a significance from the other branches, it was highlighted in many reports.

*I could not (dig) up enough studies which included the Coast Guard to feel right about adding them to the list. The small amount of studies indicated the risk was in line with the lower end of the three branches, but still did not get the significant lower risk factor, as depicted in the studies, like the Air Force.

There is a very high risk associated with the consumption of alcohol and sexual assaults, whether it was consumed by the perpetrator, victim or both. The military, as a whole, sponsors the use of alcohol, even to intoxication, so much so that it is considered normal to head to the bottle when you get off of work. This normalization is detrimental to the mission as a whole, as well as huge risk factor for sa/sh, but it seems to not be addressed by the branches.

I was watching a Defense Centers of Excellence webinar about health issues, affecting women service members and veterans, and I was floored. I could not believe it, so much so I had to print out part of the transcript. It was Dr. Ritchie, Chief Clinical Officer, Department of Behavior Health. She was retired from the Army. I know there are many avenues to look at when discussing sexual assault, but, I wanted…okay, just read on.

"In the area of sexual assault, we often see that the victim had prior risk factors of impulsiveness, prior history of sexual or physical abuse, maybe poor socioeconomic upbringing, poor boundaries in the home, alcohol, drug use, perhaps a marginal soldier – and this goes into the next part, which is the sexual predators who may pick their victims because they've got some vulnerabilities. Often these happen in remote locations where there's nobody to confide in. And then afterwards the person often is too worried to tell or worries that they'll get into trouble."

Yes, you read exactly what was copied off the transcript. She is totally blaming the victim for their impulsiveness (which can be attributed to age and not necessarily a character flaw); previously being a victim; what social class they grew up in; dysfunctional childhood family life; alcohol use; drug use; and barely making it as a solider. So basically, let's make sure that we accredit with factors, which have no cause and effect for the abuse, to the victim. Especially when many of them had absolutely no control or responsibility for. Risk factors or not, they are not responsible for being sexually assaulted! There is only one difference between a victim who had some, or all of these factors and someone who was not assaulted – the decision of the perpetrator.

You can be clinically impulsive and it does not cause assaults. You be a victim over and over, but this also does not cause an assault. You could have grown up in an extremely impoverished neighborhood and it does not cause an assault. Your childhood family could have coined the term – dysfunctional, but it does not cause an assault. No use of any substance, legal or not is the cause of an assault. You could have made Private Benjamin look like a totally squared-away soldier and this still would not have brought about the assault. I do not understand why it seems to be so hard for many of the leaders to wrap their heads around the fact that the cause of a sexual assault and sexual harassment is the choice of the perpetrator. How about let us start to punish them for what they have done? It actually is a great deterrent. Try it, it really does work.

"Having said that, I think they both end up as victims, because a guy who's charged with rape or sexual assault, most of the time, he's going to leave as well, even if he's found not guilty at a court-martial, but it's going to be out. And if convicted, of course, he's going to go to jail for felony, and he's going to have a hard problem with a career anywhere...."

After I heard this, I had to use grounding, then breathing techniques, then music, and then more positive coping skills were enlisted. Oh, yea, let's feel sorry for this poor guy who cannot get a job because all he did was "something?" How about let the guy feel grateful that he is not dead! I am not here to mix words. I have no respect for this alleged victim advocate, but I can totally see her sitting with the perp concocting the strategy of tearing apart the victim's character, and playing the 'poor nice guy' card in a court room. When this is the leadership, how are we supposed to react? When would any of us want to disclose when faced with that type of idioticy.

> *Although the world is full of suffering,*
> *it is also full of the overcoming of it. –*
> *Helen Keller*

Self-Blame & Guilt

I lived in the city and went to pick up my kids. I left my purse in my vehicle and I went into the building. When I came back outside it was stolen. I should have known better. Not only do I blame myself, but I accept others accusations of me too. Am I right? Who leaves their purse in the car in a city? Well I should not indict myself. It was ultimately the choice of the person who stole my purse which caused the theft. It was not the purses fault. It was not that it was left. It was not where we were. Although any one of them is a risk factor, it was the choice made by someone else that caused this.

Now for the rest of the details. The city population was under 18,000, not really what most would place under the term 'city,' but it is a city. My children were at our church for youth group. The church does not sit on a busy street, but residential and when you enter the parking lot the building is at the far end. There is only one way to get in and out of the parking lot. There is a high wooden fence along the side of the church, a hill to the other and woods with kind of a swampy grass grounds (you just don't walk back there). There is a parking lot around the entire building, and it is completely lit. It is a small ward, so everybody knows everybody and if there is someone unknown, they surely will welcome them and ask who they are there for, or how we can help. There were cars and people all over. I parked under one of the light poles with one parking spot open on the both sides of me, and cars in front of me. I had locked all the doors and windows were rolled up. I wasn't gone into the building very long. My purse was under my jacket on the floor behind the passenger side seat. All my windows are tinted. At the time, I carried a normal backpack, like one a high school student would have; it was my purse. My vehicle was an SUV with "K-9 Search & Rescue" on the sides. The passenger side window was smashed and the doors all unlocked to search for my purse. With all of that does it now make a difference in the responsibility part? Has whatever percentage of responsibility you might have placed on me, from the first, been taken a little off and placed back on the thief?

It was a crime of opportunity. Not only a crime of opportunity, but from someone who knew me personally. Knew me well enough to know what my purse looked like and where I put it when I got in the vehicle. Since nobody seemed to see what happened, it also was someone who was attending the youth group. More than likely a teenager from the bold and brazen smashing of the window.

We all make bad decisions, and of course at the time they do not have to be seen as bad. How many times have you or someone you know left their purse in the car to just run in and get something? Only when it was stolen did my decision become bad. Had nothing happened, I would not have thought it to be a preposterous decision. I really did envisage (visualize) the purse would be safe. Had the same risk factors been in place, except for the person who knew me, the risk of my purse actually getting stolen that night would had dropped so low it wouldn't have been measureable. That is what the perp brings to the situation, the unknown, which can make the risk go from tiny to opportunity. So why blame yourself? Can you see inside a person's head, read their thoughts, and know what they are thinking?

A question I ask all the time, if you had known what was going to happen, would you have: Walked down that road? Taken that offered ride? Gotten drunk? Said yes to the date? Turned left? Turned right? Just enter in whatever it is you think it was. The answer I always get is no. And if the answer is no, then at the time, whatever choice you made was with all the information you had at that point. Your actual choice would have been taking the left instead of a right – neutral decision. You could have taken that right and still been assaulted, it wasn't the direction that caused it. Here's another question – don't you think someone has been in a similar situation and did not get sa/sh? The alteration? It was the perv's choice! Women have been drunk, on drugs, out late, barely dressed, said all sorts of things, acted all sorts of ways – and not all of them were sa/sh. The "it's not you, it's him/her" really is true here. It wasn't you, it was him.

Along with self-blame, you can reflect back on the experience wondering, "What if I had done this differently?" This can be compounded when you also have people asking why you did or did not do something. You can fixate on what you did, on what you assume to be the reasons for the assault, and/or what you think you could have done that would have changed the outcome. Although you might say that it was the perpetrator who committed the offense, you may believe you had some responsibility in what occurred. It is not your behaviors which define sa/sh; it is the actions of the offender.

Why is it that when the 'what if' comes out, the outcome is thought of always in the positive? Maybe nothing would have happened, or the next night you went out again, walking across the road and you were hit by a drunk driver and died? There is no worth is wasting time or mental energy on 'what if's.' They are not just positive fantasy-thinking; they actually are another form of self-blame. The 'what if,' can easily be changed with "I could've, should've, would've" – self-blame.

Guilt

Guilt is a necessary feeling hopefully prompting you to repentance after you have sinned. It is having the awareness of accountability, the remorse for, the commission of – a wrong, sin, violation, crime, etc. When you feel guilty, you are taking on the responsibility, which in your case is inappropriately placed and not yours. Whatever moral sins you committed, the sa/sh was not a part of any of that. Thankfully for any sin that was committed, our Lord and Savior, Jesus Christ, paid for it, all we have to do is to go to Him with a broken heart, contrite spirit and fully repent.

One of the emotional readings that MST survivors possess, is feelings of guilt, so they assume that indicates they must be responsible for the sa/sh, or at least some molecule of responsibility. Even if you feel guilty, it is not factual, that guilt is misplaced, you have no blameworthiness for any fragment of the sa/sh; therefore; your perception of guilt is erroneous (inaccurate). What emotions/feelings do you have that you habitually accept to be accurate about yourself?

But if a man find a betrothed damsel in the field, and the man force her, and lie with her: then the man only that lay with her shall die: - Deut. 22:25-26

Just One of the Guys

I like to watch people. It is not creepy; I study human behavior and it's fascinating. In the military it was no different, and there were so many more people from all over. It was not until after Basic that I was hit head on with how much any feminine words were synonymous with revolting; I had joined a predominately male field. In the new ultra-macho, gladiatorial arena, the entirety of my being, was condemned. This propelled several outlandish Neanderthalish behaviors, of a few women, to be embraced. I have noticed the more time spend in the military, especially within traditionally male career fields more women camouflaged their femininity, to various intensities, whether they did it consciously or unconsciously.

I personally knew ones who morphed to be 'just one of the guys.' Not just wanted, as I did, but changed, even their disposition. But I really did not want to be a guy. I wanted the opportunity they had, that I did not. The opportunity of not having my very gender mocked as worthless. I surmised if I just did my best, always, then I would be seen as an asset and taken out of the 'female classification' and into 'just one of the guys' ranks. It did not work that way. The more I perfected, the further I was loathed by the majority.

I also noticed that more sexual attention I got, the less and less I would fix up myself for work. I realized what I was doing and quickly stopped. I knew I would never be seen as just one of the guys. Eventually, I pinpointed that I didn't want to be, I wanted to be respected, as they automatically afforded one another. I was a woman and wholly actualized, of not just what I'd accomplished, but who I was, which always began as female.

The first was becoming a Security Policeman, then gaining the Military Working Dog Handler status, (another reason to be hated), with more jokes of how I achieved that. It just continued: excellence in CDCs; outstanding in EOC; excellent in 5ᵗʰ level; Letters of Appreciation; SAC Superior Performer; Certificates of Appreciation; Letters of Accommodation; Medals; ribbons; stars on ribbons; and more. The more attention I was getting from outside the squadron, the more negative attention I was getting from the inside of the squadron. All of what I did was countered with: sexual discrimination; sexual harassments; sexual assaults; Letters of Counseling; Letters of Reprimand; an Article 15, and eventually a

General Discharge 39-10, Pattern of Minor Disciplinary Infractions (the easy way to say you really didn't do anything wrong – we just don't like you).

Let me talk about my 'fictitious' friend. The predominate one - 'Lauri' (names changed). Lauri dumped everything "girlish" (as she called it), she was not that girly-girl to start with, but I watched how her demeanor deepened, swore more, talked about sex, wanted to fight. She wanted to be seen as a guy. The guys did not accept her at all. She was allowed to exchange filthy sex stories, and once she left they joked about her. I was not in their group, but they also weren't very quiet, so just being near them (and at times I had to) I got an ear full. She acted tough – the "bring it on" – so they did. Sure she was scrappy, but most men and women are constructed differently, men have much more upper body strength. She got hurt a lot, really hurt. The more she tried the more they abused her, used her, out right vicious – and she took it thinking that she was being treated as one of the guys. She thought that up until the day they left her high and dry. All that to be set up for a serious fall.

I am not really bursting any one's bubble but it is imperative to be said – women and men are not the same, we were created differently but are still equals in God's eyes. We should not be camouflaging our womanhood. There is nothing to be ashamed about because we are all daughters of our Heaven Father. It is not that we do not have the brain power or capabilities but the answer is not to leave behind our birthright as women, but to be who we are, and to live up to our divine potential.

Each of us in equally valued in the eyes of the Lord. – Bonnie Oscarson

---

Sometimes after an assault we assign a feminine attribute to the reason for it and begin to camouflage our femininity. If we have on any level, in an attempt to become one of the guys, it can spiral to entire characteristic transformation, not out of wanting to fit in, but out of survival. Yes being a woman is the high risk factor for sa/sh, but your womanish attributes are not.

Think about your character prior to the military, and if assaulted before the military, if there was a time that you were allowed to be the type of girl you wanted to be. Or just the type of girl you (wanted to be) but never got to. What was she like? Did she wear cute little dressed and bows? T-shirts and jeans with sparkling fingernail polish? Face, hair, nails, heels, and dress? There is nothing wrong with any of the above done modestly. There also is nothing wrong with not liking any of it either. What you should ask yourself is, why this and not that?

You can take small steps to return or incorporate these into to your life. Even clear fingernail polish with sparkles can be a positive addition. Think about what you visualize when you hear the words: woman, lady, girl and female. Has it changed from before the military? I read a posting where someone wrote that the word 'lady' was derogatory, then another where female was also. When I was low crawling with my M-16 through the sand, a boot pushed me down into it, and I heard "keep your butt down, Airman, you crawl like a girl." I replied "I am a girl, sir!" And was proud of that.

Glitter is tiny magical specks of laughter. – Me

Trust and Betrayal

Prior to the military I really did not consider what it was like to trust my life to someone else. After 18 years, I had what I would consider a normal level of trust, for that age. I had not seen the horrific acts one human could purposely commit upon another with joyfulness and total willingness. I did have a small town girl's naive ideology, that the military, especially my career field of law enforcement, would walk a super tight line.

In Basic Training it was trust your bed-buddy (yea, stupid word but that's what it was called, now wingman/battle buddy). I made life-friends, the ones where years can go by without any contact but if I got a call that help was needed, I would help, no questions asked. The more training, the more friends, the more I trusted. The more the military had me do, the more I was forced to trust. I thought I was really good at reading who I could trust and who I had to watch, and there were a lot of people I had to watch.

Trust is a huge issue. I find it disheartening to see many programs which say they are for MST survivors not hit on this subject, or not discuss it in depth. One of the unique circumstances with experiencing MST is the level and intensity of trust betrayal. Depending on the relationship you had with the abuser does have an impact on the level(s) of trust, which were violated. Along with that, there can be many more levels of betrayal.

All levels of trust can be impacted after an assault. You may doubt your ability to trust your own feelings or to be able to manage things. Doubt your confidence in people or the world in general. Opening up to any person, no matter how insignificant the information is, can make you feel totally vulnerable. You may have thoughts that everyone has some hidden agenda behind their actions, especially ones that seem out of their way to be nice to you. Trust can seem to be an all-or-nothing concept, you either trust or you do not. But trust is more like on a continuum. You can trust your own feelings, other peoples, and the world, but each on its own specific level for the situation. Trusting any one person 100% is extremely unusual and could point to an inability to set appropriate boundaries, instead of actual trust. There are aspects to trust – how much you think the person is trustworthy and how much you are able to trust.

Most people do not realize how much trust they put into others on a daily basis. You trust the electricity company to keep your lights on, trust when you have breakfast, that the milk you drink really is milk. But what most describe for trust is actually in the confidence or strength given or relied upon to another. After an assault, your ability to trust others, have true confidence in their capability, can diminish down to a very few, if any. Some even stop trusting all together.

It was not just the violation of my body but the violation of many ideals I had. Did you think like I did? That in the military, people, especially higher ups and law enforcement, would be sticklers for following procedures? I assumed the system would have in place procedures and laws to help out victims of any crime. I presumed because someone was a supervisor, trainer, NCO, officer, they would have a moral code. If everything failed, I thought that I would be backed by my peers. Those and many more are the possible violations of trust. There were laws, but that did not stop most. Just because the military said a person could be a supervisor, did not mean they should. Just because they were in that position, it did not bequeath to them more of a sense of duty, respect, honor, and so forth. Unfortunately, many of my fellow law enforcement officers (not using officer as a rank but a title), were horrible people. We were given a lot of power, for most at a very young age, with the ability to get away with most things. I do not know why the Air Force allows anyone who can make it into the military to be Security Police (now called Security Forces). I actually thought that my career field would weed out people with obvious character flaws and criminal behavior. Ones which wanted power and wanted to abuse it. With questionable morals, in it all for themselves. Wow, was I wrong. Security Police seemed to be the dumping ground for others who could not make it in other fields.

These levels of betrayal can be difficult to understand and explain. Most MST survivors are violated by someone personally known to them, usually in the chain of command, and at times having to depend on them for safety and security. This feeling is one of more than treachery by some coworker, civilian supervisor or boss, it has an impression of incest. The perpetrators did not only betray the trust they were given from the system, they betrayed the trust you gave them. I assumed if I thought back, trying to see what red flags were there to tell me this person was not trustworthy, to identify them, so if I came upon them again I would see them The assumption was I would not be assaulted.

My supervisor, SSgt Odell who assaulted me, had been a co-worker, supervisor and I presupposed a friend. This was the first predator that had put me in his cross hairs. He was: in charge of how long; what days; what times; where I worked; and even could deny me leaving the compound (which he did); post me with guys who would not back me up (which he did); work me every day (which he did); call me off my post to "talk" with him (as he did) refuse my requests to leave the compound, (as my supervisor, I had to ask permission to leave the compound on my off-duty time); ground me to the compound (as he did); change my living quarters (which he did to isolate me); call me back to the compounds on my off-duty time to "talk" (as he did), and more. He literally could post me on posts which were more dangerous than others, cause more pain, and did. That is a level of betrayal that can be so painstaking to interpret for others, mostly civilians. I had trusted him with my life and he took that trust and abused it to his own gratification, his own predatory will.

It has been difficult to slowly allow others trust, and I would say there are only a few people who I really trust. I trust nobody completely and when I meet someone new, there is no trust; they must earn it. I am very suspicious of others and still it takes a while for me to slightly open up, and I do mean slightly. So how to trust again? It is the risk factor written about before, low risk, higher safety; one small step at a time.

Trust in the Lord with all thine heart;
- Prov 3:5

6
DEFENSE MECHANISMS

Ants (Automatic Negative Thoughts)

Automatic Negative Thoughts was a term coined by Aaron Beck and referred to as "Ants." In many explanations, authors use the picnic visualization where ants come out, and if you do not deal with one of them; they get friends. I prefer to see them as fire ants. If you have ever been where there are fire ants, you know what I am talking about when I say they swarm. I see the thoughts like stepping on one of their mounds. It only looks like a little bit of ground tossed to the top, but when you even barely move their dirt, they swarm. You do not have to even step directly on the mound, just a little vibration near it. Fire ants not only sting but bite and the pain lasts a long time. It produces a blister that incessantly itches and hurts, completely maddening. You can even end up in the hospital from them. That is how these Ants are. It's not some pretty picnic and you just shoo them away, at the most move your blanket over, nope. They have friends, lots of friends, and can cause injuries, pain, and scars.

All or Nothing Thinking

As with fire ants, Ants come in many different species – One such Ants category is: All or nothing thinking. It is pretty much just like it says, all or nothing. You place situations and people into only those two categories: Allness and Neverland. In allness nothing changes – "people are always the same;" "I am always the same;" and none of it is positive. "No matter how hard I try, things always will go wrong." "I always get hurt." "You always blame." "We always end up fighting." For neverland all you do is just change the wording around – "No matter how hard I try, things will never go right." "I will never be better." "We never do anything but fight," and so forth.

To counteract these thoughts, or Ants, sit yourself outside the situation, and start using facts. Does this really always happen? Yes, sometimes things do go wrong, but it is not always wrong, and if you think about it the never falls into the same situation. You can say that you do not feel you are being listened to at that time, but the never? It will be difficult since these are considered automatic, and most are not accustomed to stopping the thoughts and countering them; but it is necessary. In the beginning, writing down a list of your counters so that when the Ants come out, you do not have to try and figure what is considered a positive reply. What and/or who are you placing into Allness and/or Neverland?

Labeling

We all use labels – "I'm a jerk." "I'm just stupid." "I am a looser." Labeling yourself compacts everything that you really are into one behavior or stereotype limiting your outlook. We can do stupid things, but we are not stupid. Along with that, we also are not our diagnosis or disability. When you use these terms over and over, you begin to not only believe the label, but at times even modify your conduct to make the label true. It also has a sense of not being able to change, as though that is all you are now, and all that you will be. What labels are you using for yourself? Others?

No one can make you feel inferior
without your consent. - Eleanor Roosevelt

Negative Filtering

These Ants would retrieve the moldy sour grape from a huge buffet of rich picnic food. These Ants are when no matter what is said or experienced you pull out the negatives and focus on them. We have a tendency to ruminate on the unfavorable parts of any situation. Nothing is perfect, so in each new experience we will have something that is either negative or can be perceived as negative.

Negative filtering is taking what you would call the best day of your life and because something didn't go exactly the way you wanted it; that is all you talk about. With this type of screening there really isn't ever a good experience.

I had been asked to talk about MST at a conference. It would be my first time back in front of a lot of people after a mental health set-back episode; really far, far back. I felt it was horrible. I forgot some information, got suckered into a person's personal debate and was as nervous as I had been about 10 years ago, when I first started to talk in front of people about MST. After I sat down and began to critique myself, something I do to help with the next talk. After a while I looked at what I had wrote. I hadn't put one positive critique down; it was all critical. I took each statement and countered it with facts, not insults. These Ants are not just about your own internal thoughts but even when others are complimenting you, your reply is switched to negative. When the positive comments from others began to pour in, I had to be very focused that I did not discount them with "but I could have said," or "it would have been better if." Instead I accepted them just as they were intended, as compliments, from a job well done.

We make thousands of decisions everyday in automatic mode without a mistake. Yet we don't reflect and celebrate this wonderful mode of human decision making at work, rather we put the blow torch on the one moment when it doesn't work and something goes wrong. – Dr Rob Long

Unrealistic Expectations

In your mind these Ants won't hurt you – they're just cute little bright red guys who you can get around without being harmed. No, These Ants are placing characteristics, actions, or other out-of-reach goals on yourself, which you will always fall short of. I wanted to complete my book within a few months, and when that time frame came and I was not even one fifth into it. The Ants go marching one by one. I heard in my mind "I am not a good writer. I cannot sit down and just quickly type out dozens of pages without looking back to see if I'm using the correct citing, reference, or explanation." Completing the book in that short amount of time was an unrealistic expectation of mine. And finishing it has nothing to do with its quality (another Ants). Another example is I have never run in a marathon, and it would be an unrealistic expectation for me to set as my goal coming in first place in a national marathon in a few weeks from now. Almost everyone can see that as unrealistic, but it's the ones you tell yourself others have or I did in the past – these Ants sneak up on you.

We put so many unrealistic expectations upon ourselves and others without factoring in that whole human concept; that we set ourselves up to fail. We are not and cannot be the super mom, super wife, and super employee, so replace those unrealistic expectations. There is only a certain amount of time in the day and no amount of assumed superness will change that. This is not to stay in mediocracy or not to do your best, but pat yourself on your back for what you have done, don't degrade yourself for what you did not.

For many survivors on their journey, we employ unrealistic expectations on the time we resolve it should take to recover, that eventually our trauma will have no effect on us. We get upset at ourselves for not conquering it. We try to set and achieve a timeline to integrate some experience into our life, without any negative symptoms, as if we can put them on a timeline. This isn't a race, and everyone has their own personal healthy pace.

Psychic Reading

These are 'all knowing' Ants. They are when you already think you know what is going to happen. Pretty much trying to tell the future. You tell yourself even though you love poetry, if you go to the national poetry convention you will not have fun. You will not find anything interesting, and it will be a waste of money. Guess what? Your thoughts will most likely come true. It also includes thinking you can read the thoughts of others.

If you think you can or think you can't, you are right. - Henry Ford

---

It happens often when you are talking about your symptoms or your diagnosis as a whole. You keep things to yourself because you know that the other person is thinking – "You are just nuts." or that "You are exaggerating to get some type of attention." You certainly do not know what another person is actually thinking unless they tell you. Even people who have been married for years can guess what the other is probably thinking but that is not the same as knowing. If couples knew exactly what the other person was thinking, there would be a lot less divorce and couples counseling. What have you thought others were thinking about you?

What did you "know" about some event and either did or didn't go, and it was just as you thought it would be?

Emotional Reading

Right as you mistakenly step on these Ants mounds, they feel threatened. So automatically they are in attack mode, whatever the feeling, it is true. All their feelings are perceived as being fact. "I feel so useless, therefore, I am useless." Your feelings can actually lie to you; feeling some way does not make it true. There are ways in which you can change the way you feel by changing the way that you think. Have you ever noticed when you start to feel down all these negative experiences flood your mind until you are emotionally sad, those Ants! It is a downward spiral and if you do not stop yourself, you will slip down that slide all the way to the bottom, face first. Counter these thoughts with realistic thoughts and tell yourself that even if you do feel blue you do not have to think that way.

Suicidal Ideation

All traumas are difficult to get through, but there can be circumstances involved in your trauma, which, in your perspective, may seem to go beyond the want to continue to live. If you have any of these thoughts, it is crucial for you to get help, NOW. Do not ignore your own thoughts, believing they will just go away. If you are considering suicide and/or feel unsafe, call the following hotline to speak with someone, 24 hours a day - 1-800-273-8255 (1-800-273-TALK). It can be difficult to make the call, if you are having trouble you can call someone to help you, but make that call. The continuation of these thoughts usually does not end well, and are people who deeply care about your wellbeing.

I have had several attempts, but I always woke up. They were not calls out for help, or seeking any type of attention. I was not ambivalent about wanting to live or die; I wanted to die. I told nobody what I was doing, made sure I would be alone and that no one would come looking for me until it was over. But I failed, well actually succeeded to continue to live. As another veteran commented about her attempts, "I'm such a screw-up, I can't even kill myself." That is how I felt waking up, that I could not believe that I could not even kill myself right. That type of negative self-talk is like an automatic negative thought.

I have always had a plan. Mistakenly, at one time, I was truthful with the VA. Yes, I have a plan. Yes, I have the means, but what is missing on their suicide check sheet was the intent. It can be frightening to admit to another you are entertaining these dark impressions. The first things on most people's mind is "Why?" It is not the why that matters at this point. It is the immediate emergency to be helped. I did not care if I lived or died, death was okay, but I was not going to go through with the plan; there was no intent. There is a scripture that continually comes to my mind – "endure to the end." And not the "end" that I create.

I have met and communicated with many veterans who attempted suicide, as well as wives and family members of veterans who did commit suicide. Some question why someone who seemed to be hurting so much, did not talk but ended their life. Especially when the ones, who said they loved them, were continually asking if everything was okay. From my experience and others, there are a few common central themes. One of them is that we did not try to hurt anyone else, just wanted our own pain to end. We thought we had become a burden for our loved ones. I felt everyone was better off if I was gone. That it would relieve the stress on others. The continuation of their worries, their burdens of having to take care of all the chaos I manufactured. When asked why I said nothing, I still have not talked about some of the reasons I want to end my life, and I never wanted to burden my loved ones with the pictures of what I saw when I closed my eyes. I still do not want them to have any of those images in their minds. It is not that I do not want them to understand; it is that I feel I am protecting them from the demons which surrounded me. I wish that I could forget but I know that is not going to happen. I just did not want anyone else to be living in the mental purgatory that I was in.

National Suicide toll-free hot-line number:
1-800-273-TALK (8255) Press 1.
Military OneSource: 1-800-342-9647
Wounded Soldier and Family Hotline: 1-800-984-8523

This was not an attempt to punish anyone for what we were going through. We just wanted the pain to end. It had gone on for so long, it just perceived to keep getting worse. It truly is just as painful as a physical injury of being stabbed. We had begun to believe our loved ones were actually better off without us. Not that they would be glad we were gone, but that the millstone we surmised we had become, we wanted to end. Suicide was not the first thoughts, the first cry out for help, (whether we acknowledged or not that is what we needed). The first attempt was to try and fix it alone – it was a point after, we had come to the erroneous conclusion there was nothing left. We "knew" whatever we either tried next, was more of a burden, or it absolutely would not work.

Suicidal thoughts are not uncommon, and I have no shame in having had them. I have had lots of thoughts that are not good, yet I did not act upon them (a good way to stay out of prison). But even though it can start out as just one thought, these Ants are happy in colonies, and the more there are of them, the more torture ensues. I have heard the statement, "the Lord will never give you anything you cannot handle." What is vitality missing is the actual rest of the sentence, "with His help." This life was never promised to be easy or without adversity. It is not something I would advise anyone to deal with alone. I thought it – couldn't, wouldn't, and shouldn't – get better for me. I was mistaken. My Lord and Savior helped me through the blackest moments of my life. He was there for me, and will always be there for you too.

Anger

When someone says they feel anger, what do you visualize? Screaming? Storming about? Silently brooding? Face crinkled up and red? So what does anger look like to you? Is it the same as your best friends? Many words in our wacked out language have multiple meanings which causes confusions all over, this is one of them.

Anger is a powerful, normal, healthy, emotion. The chemicals which are released are warning signals. The emotion is not good or bad, right or wrong. There is no condemnation or judgement upon the emotion itself and or the person having it; it just is. As these chemicals continue to be release into the body it can decrease your sensitivity to pain and at the same time increase your strength. That rush can seem to make things much more focused and understandable.

Now you begin to feel the chemicals and interpret them as anger, or angry, depending on how you state the feeling. "I am feeling angry" or "Anger is what I feel." But that is all this anger is, a feeling. Yes, you might have increased strength and your thoughts could be racing but again it is just a feeling. When action is taken on this feeling that is no longer an emotion or a feeling, it is a behavior. Nobody has ever gotten into trouble for becoming angry. You wouldn't know if it wasn't for the behavior. So when a person says that they were angry, it can denote a hundred contrasting things. Normally, they are not referring to the torrent chemical releases from it. The notion that anger is inappropriate is so embedded in our society most try to suppress it out of embarrassment of not being able to stay in control. Keeping anger compressed is like a pressure cooker, the heat continues, the pressure goes up, a little leaks out here and there, but when the release can't keep up, it finally blows. This is not to suggest to hit a wall or scream out whenever you start to feel that build up, so that you do not eventually get to the eruption.

There are positive, productive, and non-violent discharges to this anger.

How did you handle the feelings of anger prior to your service? Did you have a short fuse? Was aggressive behavior, in some fashion, always the end result after feeling angry? Was this one of the issues in your civilian luggage, which got you into trouble prior to service? How did your childhood family demonstrate anger? What was acceptable?

Back to the playground slide. Now add the military training of someone screaming at you, with a whole bunch of other people, going up, down, then around the slide, then doing it all over. Your heart is racing. You are trying not to think about anything. Just as fast as possible, you are pushed up down and around. Sometimes you end up on your face. Sometimes on the person in front of you. Other times on your feet. No matter how you land, it is the continual push that is deep-seeded in your muscle memory. Whatever emotions are brought up are pushed into anger to get you up and over as quickly as possible. You get annoyed then angry at the person in front of you if they do not move fast enough. At the same time, if the one behind you moved too fast, bumping into you, it's that chemical release again. Once out of initial training. Your training continues the push for all emotions and feelings to be funneled into anger. This is the one, and only, emotional response that is condoned. All others are weak. So your slide is all one motion and automatic.

Upon all the above, a horrible evil was committed on you, and most likely it did not end there. After the betrayal how many more levels were you made to suffer? That is the idea, to not think. So when all your training is to focus to slide on through the anger, it's a habitual pattern. It is attached to the core survival instinct of fear. There is no thinking. It has become habitually automatic.

In one of my non-confidential online groups, anger, angry, and aggressive behavior seems to pop up continually. It starts out as someone venting about another person's driving. Wow, I am glad most of them do not have access to tanks. A comment of "They just aren't thinking," had to be responded to. I'll paraphrase what I posted – No, it starts with one thinking about themselves only. They are saying that getting to their appointment on time, work, getting home early, etc., is more important than whatever you have going on. It's not only more important than what you're doing, it's more important than your life, your passenger's lives, the lives of all those around us. If pushed to it, even my own. It's the entitlement mindset. I'm entitled to go where I want to without being disrupted by anyone else. – It was my lane, my turn and/or my right.

I personally am not a passive driver, but when I'm cut off, or someone flies up behind me, I just go on with what I was doing or wait until I can get over to let them go by. If I have already had my limit of irritability for the day (which usually means in one way or another, I had dealings with the VA), then it's to the coping skills of music and breathing techniques. There is a CD that I just smile to myself when listening to most all the songs. One of them in particular, brings up memories of my children laughing and singing along. That is my go-to, when moments get rough. Closing your eyes and trying to visualize your safe place is not a positive coping skill here, so no need to try it. I've had those nod-off drives (mostly in the military) to tell you. Just the first step of trying to utilize that skill is a doozy. As I stress – solitary coping skills do not cover all situations.

He that is slow to wrath is of great understanding: but he that is hasty of spirit exalteth folly. – Prov. 14:29

Avoidance

It is understandable a victim would want to avoid the perpetrator and the place in which the assault happened. Unfortunately, if you happen to still be in the military that avoidance can be unrealistic. If the perp happens to be a co-worker or in your chain of command, you may not only have to see them, but actually interact with them, sometimes on a daily basis. Also if the assault occurred in your sleeping quarters or work place, it is not likely you can just ask to be given another room or work somewhere else, especially if you happen to be deployed.

Many victims begin to realize that they not only avoid the assailant (if possible) and the place, but situations, settings, people, which remind them and may trigger a trauma memory. You may be able to avoid the subject of the military all together, never telling your new civilian co-workers and even new friends that you are a veteran. It can appear easier to say nothing than to respond to questions about your service. What is overlooked, is that the brain associates all sorts of stimuli with the assault. Now not only the assailant, but maybe others who resemble him, or just men in general. Possibly what he was wearing, and if it was a uniform, well you can understand that struggle, especially when seeking care at the VA.

Avoidance can lead into isolation. It is very common for MST survivors to physically, emotionally, and spiritually isolate themselves from the rest of the world. A shackle to isolation is the ability to seemly connect with others via electronic (posting, instant messaging, texting, etc.). It can be very difficult to venture out, in and around others you do not know, or places which are not familiar. However, we as humans need those connections, those in person connections (sorry social media, Facebook doesn't count).

If you have noticed your lack in wanting to be around others, it's normal, but it should be ironed out. A good start can be a controlled drop-in group program. These programs are subject or group specific – survivor groups, mental health diagnosis groups, bible study groups, disabled veterans, women veterans, women, etc. As a controlled group, people should not be coming and going during the discussions. It should have a precise starting and ending time, usually weekly on the same day at the same time, meeting in the same place. There should be a facilitator in charge of the group, and preferably two with split duties. Excluding the bible study-type groups, all participants should be required to fill out a confidentiality form. I know, I've been to the groups that do this and right after you hear someone in the parking lot discussing what was said to another on the phone, but more people will comply, if there is an official printed form they must fill out.

Avoidance can also be a hindrance to getting help. Although the VA offers free counseling and other services related to the effect of experiencing MST, the atmosphere oozes military. It is predominately male patients and many proudly display their previous branch, unit, career field, conflict, or just wear their old service jackets. But advoiding all things qusi- military, limits a possible resource from your backpack. Are there people, places, issues that you are avoiding because of your sa/sh? You may not be aware you are dodging them, it is worthwhile to ask another person if they have observed issues you seem to skirt around (make sure this person is trustworthy).

Do you tend to stay at home more often?

The greatest healing therapy is friendship and love. – Hubert H. Humphrey

Depression

As with other emotions on the emotional continuum, sadness can escalate from gloomy to clinical depression. When the symptoms do not conform to the criteria, for any of the depressive disorders, it can be a symptom of another disorder or its own emotional feeling. Even mild forms of depression have this cyclonic inability to move yourself out, without professional assistance. The professional help can be medication or psychotherapy or a combination of both, but external intervention is essential.

Depression isn't just a sad day, or the blues, even mild depression is more than that. Although people say they are depressed, most often they are just deeply saddened, another term we have thrown around so much that when someone truly is depressed, others dismiss it.

There are many signs and symptoms of depression. Do you:
- Feel tired for most of the day?
- Don't take pleasure in things you used to?
- Have trouble concentrating?
- Feel like crying all the time?
- Nothing seems to make you laugh?
- Do you lack energy?
- Blame yourself?
- Feel worthless?
- Having physical symptoms without medical explanation?
- Have a feeling of not caring, or no feelings at all?
- Do not see a future for yourself?
- Believe things will not get better no matter what?
- Feel agitated all the time?
- Feel like nobody understands or cares?
- Others ask me what is wrong and say that I should probably talk with someone.

- Do you feel isolated?
- Sleep longer than normal?
- Have thoughts that your loved ones would be better off if they did not have to take care of you?

The more of the above questions that you can answer yes to, the more likely you are depressed.

Sorrow looks back with sadness. Worry looks up and down, from side to side, with fear. Faith looks forward with hope and gladness. – Anonymous

---

Emotional Numbing

Extreme numbness has been described as a shutting down of all emotions relating to the trauma and life. You can either begin to briefly start to feel and then shut them down. Or it's become habit and before your consciousness is aware of the difference, the switch has been turned off. In a mild form, you do not experience emotions about the trauma in general, but can have feelings like anger and sadness about other concerns. However, love and tender affections most often are not sensed. In the extreme degree, you have no emotions at all. It can feel like being disconnected from the world and/or your body. Things you once enjoyed doing and interests you, no longer seem to have any meaning, they are not enjoyable. Many wonder how they can have no feelings when others around them, family and friends, seem to be experiencing guilt, anger, and sadness. When you are emotionally disconnected, you can talk in considerable detail or write about the trauma without batting an eye. Although this might be interpreted from others or even yourself, as the experience not being a trauma, or as others would say "not that bad," or that you have "gotten over it," and "moved on;" this is false. Numbing does not indicate that you were not traumatized, and/or that the above listed emotions are not slowly leaking out. Continually repressing these emotions may mean that someday they could just explode.

Emotional numbing may occur along with a physical experience of pins and needles, alienation, detachment from others, and/or feelings of being in a dreamlike state of unreality. Mentally a person can have impaired concentration, inability to make decisions, amnesia, inability to plan future action, and/or confusion. An emotionally numb person would have a flat affect. As an individual you can learn to fake appropriate behavioral responses, in social settings, in an attempt to disguise your inability to feel. Theories behind why a person would become numb, or split in two, has been said to be an initial survival technique. Even at that, continual numbing about the incident is a defense mechanism. It keeps you from being able to accept what has occurred and to integrate the event into your life.

Emotional numbness can be a constant state or situational. At the VA, I notice a turning off of that switch, when I began to seek medical treatment there. It seemed to be an emotional avalanche every time I walked in. There was the annoyance of waiting in line while clerks talked, did other work, and ignored us. Once people got to the desk the snotty and quick cut-you-off comebacks were spewed. Then it would continue to the "Mr. Wells, Mr. Wells," rebuffing my veteran status, and making it very apparent they did not even glance at my medical slip in their hands. After the misunderstanding of gender was over another nurse was at times called, as if there is a difference between taking the blood pressure, temperature and weight of a woman. Back to the sitting area to wait, and wait, and sometimes still wait more. Another nurse, another question about gender, then into the doctors room and wait, again.

This was normal procedure. Depending on the reason for my appointment, annual checkup; another annual prostate exam (After the second one I was sent to, I thought about filling out a disability claim. Apparently I was missing parts.); something I'd never heard about but VA required it; or I had requested the appointment. The purpose made substantial impact on how the appointment went. It could be quick and painless or full of stumbling blocks, miscommunications, egotism, and frustrations. It was too much to govern all at once, so I had to quash (suppress, squelch) all emotions. It took a while but I did learn how to manage these emotions/feelings when they occurred.

There were times I went to the clerk and ask for somewhere private I could wait. Apparently she thought I was joking, but I just stood there until they found me another area. It was either that or out the door, and have to reschedule (which I had probably already waited months to get that appointment).

Flashbacks

Flashbacks is a psychological term of a particular type of vivid intrusive memory. Whatever response the flashback comes in, what and how many of your senses are hijacked, it is more like re-living the initial trauma. The response is intrusive, in that you did not try to remember it and that perception is drawing you away from the here and now. Having a flashback can cause you a sense of panic, that these emotions are recurring, and you cannot control them. There usually is a trigger causing the flashbacks; however trying to pinpoint it can be difficult. Flashbacks not only remove the sense(s) from here and now but reinforces the original trauma, repetitively linking the two.

Flashbacks can be considered partial or full experience from brief episodes to 'quasi-delusional' state. They can be pieces of the trauma, which are visual, auditory, aromatic or tactile, and intrude into the mind without the person consciously trying to bring them up. It is not just a thought or memory with some emotions attached. You are reliving the trauma, mind, body, and soul. These are more than just vivid memories, they can cause a surge of intrusive emotions; anger, confusion, rage, shame, and vulnerability. Because of the random nature of flashbacks, it can be difficult to make logic of them, or even realize what possibly triggered them in the first place. A sight of a red coat, the smell of a certain perfume, even the small smile of a stranger can trigger a flashback. It can take the person right back to the time of the trauma; to the emotions of fear, helplessness, and terror as if they are re-experiencing it all again.

I was walking down the road in East Texas. It was humid. The foliage was extensive. Just as I rounded a corner, I was right back in Panama, walking Kennel Row. I could hear the distinctive sounds of rainforest wildlife. It was sensed just for a brief second then I was back. It was considerably unnerving. I swore I was there, could feel the boots under my feet, the heaviness of BDU's on my body, but I was looking at my road in Texas. Although I was visually back to the here and now, the chemicals had already been released. My arms tightened. The hairs on the back of my neck stood up. It took a considerable amount of time to let the emotions just flow through. I acknowledged what had ensued, which logically permitted me to fare the experience but the awareness of being hijacked was still worrisome.

When I'm having any sensory flashback, my first pulled-out skill, from my backpack is grounding. Using as many senses as I can to seize back to this here and now. I fashioned a 'Battle Buddy' as I call them. I found if I merge my senses, I recoup rapidity. I made a small German Shepherd out of llama and alpaca fiber and added a dog pack to it with aroma therapy beads inside. This small replica of Killer (my MWD) produces reactions of gratefulness and unconditional love. I can caress his fur, smell the aroma beads and since I used a crinkle in the dog pack, I can hear it. He's small enough to be tucked away in my hand and stays in my purse. It worked for me so well I did my own clinical trials, without the clinical side. Everyone not only loved the animals, it undoubtedly benefited. So I added them to my therapeutic website side, JustCrafty.com; where again, all proceeds go to veteran women and MST Survivors.

Fear thou not; for I am with thee: be not dismayed; for I am thy God: I will strengthen thee; yea, I will help thee; yea, I will uphold thee with the right hand of my righteousness. - Isaiah 41:10

Hypervigilance

To be vigilant is to be keenly watchful in sensing danger. It can depend on the locality, as to what one person views as vigilance; however, to be hypervigilant goes beyond just a little jumpy. Hypervigilance, with all these heightened senses, is an increased state of anxiety with intensified sensitivity (always being on guard). Behaviors, which can include: a high response to stimuli (easily startled), significantly increased arousal (heart rate quickens), as the mind is constantly scanning the environment (always on the lookout), and you become intensely aware trying to discern danger. All these senses are heightened and it is almost as if you are expecting danger, not just trying to be cautious. This defense mechanism is an above reasonable checking or watchfulness of one's environment and does not have to be related to any realistic threat. It is an automatic response, to the unpredictable dangers, which the body already continually heightened, is watching out for.

Taking from one of my Texas friends, "you can feel like a cat in a room full of rocking chairs."

Scary movies are great to help try and explain these reactions to someone. Use the situation where the heroine is at the ball. She anticipates the villain could be there. She is walking around looking, watching, anticipating. Everybody is wearing masks so she cannot ascertain who the villain is from anyone else. The door opens and her head quickly snaps in that direction, a couple enter, but again she does not know if either of them is there for the party or to do harm. As you watch you begin to take on her acuteness and if the movie theater door opens it can have half the people scream and the other half jump. That's the feeling – logic may continually tell you, "You are in a movie theater." But your body does not signify it is listening to your logical mind, it's feeding off the fictitious sensing of danger. A vast majority love horror movies because they get that quick short-term hyper-alertness rush. But to constantly live that way, sucks the emotional and physical energy out of you.

Just from being law enforcement, I no longer like to be seated with my back toward anything but a wall. I was trained when entering a building to search for the exits, seek out oddities and watch the behavior of others. This added onto my other experiences makes being in public an anxious affair. I do not like big crowds. I actually do not like small crowds either, where I do not know anyone. I continually watch others, look for the exits, check locks, windows, and doors. I am better, but I can be sitting there and just get those hairs standing on the back of my neck – seemly for no reason. There was a trigger, what is was and how it's related, I sometimes don't know – but if I can just pinpoint it, or the circumstance in which it happened; I can gradually condition myself by means of coping skills, to rectify it. I still might get the initial feeling, but a quick logical risk assessment and onto a coping skill.

I had acquaintances think it was humorous to watch me jump, purposely making a loud noise. No matter how much I tried to explain to some, it was best to not associate with them anymore. Some needed a more direct approach. When I first got out of the military it took a while to remind myself where I was; that I no longer had that job. It took time to get to where I could start enjoying life again. I have over compensated for some of my friends, who have never even been in a car accident. They seemed not just clueless, but outright stupid, in how vulnerable they were making themselves. I use a logical risk assessments for the situation I am presently in. I still see some of the ways they seem oblivious to any threat, but I know they aren't purposely taking these risks. Their assessments are just not as vivid and experience-packed as mine.

A tremendous advantage has been having dogs at home. Not just purse accessories, but real dogs, German Shepherds. I became a fan of them when I got my first German Shepherd MWD. Sure there are dogs that have better capabilities of smell, better hearing, better eye sight, more aggressive, but overall the German Shepherd rates high across the entire board. Yes I'm bias. Dogs are not only good deterrents, their ability to perceive danger can be comforting. I can discern their contrasting 'alarm barks.' Whether it is some new cat crossing our yard, to an actual person near the fence. One must, they ought to be obedience trained. A trained dog is a happy dog. There isn't anything charming or funning about a dog jumping up on you, unless given permission. I know if someone gets into my house, the extra time I have will be helpful. It gives me a sense of more security, as well as knowing these bad guys aren't going to get much farther than meeting my dogs. And at the same time, when I am on edge, just reaching over and petting their fur can slowly decrease the anxiety; it is extremely therapeutic.

> *Do not anticipate trouble or worry about what may never happen. Keep always in the sunlight. – Benjamin Franklin*

Nightmares

Nightmares are not reserved for children and movies, many adults and especially sexual assault survivors have them. These are not just scary dreams but nightmares, heart-racing, fear-invoking content which can revolve around the trauma. This content tends to be associated around the original threat or circumstances, whether metaphorically or literally. These nightmares may also have an alternative ending than the original trauma, causing you to question your memory, and/or increase the anxiety originally felt.

Nightmares can occur more than once during the night, and you may have repeating ones, or repeating themes. Some individuals begin to act out in their dreaming state, physically moving their bodies around increasing the fatigue usually associated with frequent nightmares. It can feel as though you never slept. If left untreated, these restless nights will drastically begin to effect your ability to function – sleep deprivation.

I've read numerous times the theory behind dreaming is to work through some unresolved issues. I guess that burrito weighing on my stomach was an unresolved issue because it causes the Taco Toss – night of uncomfortable flipping, and repetitively waking up with vivid dreams, usually being eaten by other food. I can see the reasonableness behind unresolved issues, and the Taco Toss, but my dream content, and especially nightmares have been chemically induced too. A private (okay not anymore) joke between my husband and I is about the way medication labels are worded. One said "for moods," so he'd hand me the bottle and say "do you need a mood?" The best is for nightmares. The nightmare one was right on spot – if I took them, I got a nightmare, every single time. Even though the doctor continually told me I should just try again, I learned that when my body tells me something, it knows a little more than the VA doctor – Yes, it was causing increased and completely vivid nightmares without the ability to get scared and wake up – hence I have been killed all sorts of ways. By what I ingest (food wise) I can alter my dreams and nightmares. Unfortunately, I have not yet figured out how to control what the alter is, by the food. If I wanted to have a nightmare – not that I ever would, there is a combination that'll cause one, but it messes with my whole system. Or just take a pill for nightmares – that does the trick.

One way to prepare for nightmares is to have a dream log. It can be a notebook and pen put by the side of your bed (they work the best for me). You have a dream – once you're awake quickly bullet point the main events and just one word feelings. If you have time now, write what you dreamt about, the sights, smells, feedings, and any thoughts. This is for the dream that's just weird or silly. If it's disturbing or a nightmare, there are different ways to attack them. Weigh the amount of distress it caused you. As with everything dreams and nightmares are on a continuum and you are the one who draws the lines of disruption.

Start writing, when it gets to a point you begin to think differently, start to feel the tingle, or observe your hands twitching, and mouth tighter, any alteration, stop. This is where you are the author, you will guide your mind and writing to what you want. A very brief example is again my nemeses – eight-legged freak. It is either not real, or maybe a bug, a daddy long-leg (actually not a spider, non-venomous, a myth it is deadly, eight legs but in a different category – and I'm pretty much okay with them – now).

Back on topic, going further, the spider had jumped on my leg, so the bug, or whatever I've decided to make it, jumped on my leg. By the way, I have no problems with most bugs. Do not substitute one fear for another. I change the nightmare up enough and read it over a few times, visualizing it. My writer's cut is pushing the other out. If necessary I may read and visualize it during the day and right before bed again. There are the critics who state it is essential to make the spider wear a tutu and dance – yea, that maybe funny to them, all I see is The Dance of Death – in a tutu. This is all up to you. I have accepted this is how I have conquered my spider nightmare – they now fall mostly into the 'just disturbing dream part.' I've had other, more life-impeding nightmare issues to work through, eventually the spider may be able to wear a tutu, still don't think it's cute or funny. I don't think I have that good of an imagination.

I try to use as much of the details of the nightmare that don't have an emotional response attached to them. At first if the color is just that a color, use it. I have found trying to just have the beginning in common, you walk into the room, and the rest is inconsistent, doesn't do it for me. It may for you. For me, and for many I've spoken with, the more details which are the same, the quicker the symptoms seem to resolve. I would discuss this with your therapist or do some research reading first.

Yea, though I walk through the valley
of the shadow of death, I will fear no evil:
for thou art with me: they rod and they
staff they comfort me. – Palms 23:4

Somatic

Somatic symptoms are symptoms which deal with the physical body. Many studies conducted have correlated experiences of military sexual trauma with poor mental and physical health, compared with other veterans of the same era. The most common reported afflictions are headaches, unexplainable pain, fatigue, gastrointestinal difficulties, sexual dysfunction, suddenly increased heart rate, and parts of the body suddenly going numb. This can alter the chemical balance and wreak havoc all over your mind, body, and spirit.

While I was researching I came across a review which I really enjoyed the abstract of, although it was for PTSD, since that is the predominant mental diagnosis given to survivors, I just had to add it.

"Post-traumatic stress disorder (PTSD) is associated with both (1) 'ill-defined' or 'medically unexplained' somatic syndromes, e.g. unexplained dizziness, tinnitus and blurry vision, and syndromes that can be classified as somatoform disorders (DSM-IV-TR); and (2) a range of medical conditions, with a preponderance of cardiovascular, respiratory, musculoskeletal, neurological, and gastrointestinal disorders, diabetes, chronic pain, sleep disorders, and other immune-mediated disorders in various studies" (Review of Somatic Symptoms, 2013).

Wow! Seems overwhelming, right? It's not meant to be used that way. The mind can be a wonderful thing and can also be completely maddening. However, as I told a VA mental health "professional" once- "it would be a little hard to live without." We are all women, but we are not medically, chemically and/or, genetically identical. Some people can take the sleeping pill that causes nightmares for me and it just helps with their sleep, no nightmares. As one extremely smart VA doctor said "it isn't called practice for nothing." There are so many diverse variables between people, it's amazing we have the medications we do, that work. So it is reasonable that your somatic symptoms from experiencing MST could be all over the board too.

Since mental health is a whole body health, any mental health issues can disrupt other parts of the body. If you're not trying to keep out as many toxins as reasonable, those other chemicals-released symptoms will continually disrupt your whole health balance. Toxins are basically slowly decreasing your life-span, and opening you up to be bombarded from outside detrimental substances. It is like already having a sprained ankle and deciding to run a marathon. Your ankle may hurt, but eventually it will extend to the knee then maybe the other leg compensating from favoring. These somatic symptoms are as real as any physical symptoms from physical injuries.

When or if you hear someone say "it's all just in your head," tell them they are right, that's where all of it is processed at. A migraine is all in your head too, but when you get one, you're not going to just shaking it off, you have to first take precautions, then have a plan. You can take medications and wait until it either goes away, or you find stronger meds. You might have to go into a dark room; making sure it's quiet and lay down until the pain passes. Nobody can see a migraine but if you tell anyone you have one they are understandable. How many of your friends get headaches? Migraines? How do you think they would react if they had a headache or migraine and you told them, "why don't you positively talk it out, it's just a headache (migraine)" You would expect them to be shocked, it's real pain, even if it can't be seen, just as yours are.

We blast ourselves with so much negative self-talk about issues that just are, it is much better to discern them, face them, plan for them, and when or if they happen, activate your plan. People who have recurrent migraines, usually have a plan, such as I have. This plan has variations when the beginning steps do not alleviate or lessen the pain. It starts with a prescription and then into my dark room, lay down and try to wait it out. Also in my plan is preventatives. To make my plan, I researched migraines, and educated myself about everything I could, especially triggers most others have. I did a migraine log and found some of my triggers and eliminated the ones I had complete control over. And already knew they were bad, but tasted oh so good. I began to limit my interactions with the other triggers, as much as I could.

Unfortunately, a major trigger is perfumes and cigarette smoke (cigar too). With perfume it is usually the level of bathing the person did with it, but some just are complete irritating. Limiting my exposure to them is very difficult. I have had to entirely change my life. It is imperative for me to anticipate their occurrence when out, so I restrict at what times I go, less people less risk of exposure. It is difficult to be respectable of other's choices, when those choices don't effect just them. If a person just smells like smoke I move away, but when they are puffing along, walking in the parking lot, or standing right outside a door, it really gets to me. It's extremely inconsiderate of others to stand by the front of a public building and puff away. It's not just for me because I get sick when I get that into my lungs, it's for everyone else who chooses to not smoke. Church can be horrific. I situation myself to be far from the masses but sometimes I just have to leave. It can be considerably frustrating to leave a place when I've spent time getting ready for it, or am excited about attending, but that is my new reality.

Some somatic symptoms are intensified unknowingly by our own ignorance. Ignorance is not stupid, it is just uninformed – as my Texan friends say – "You can't fix stupid." Investigate your physical and mental environment.

> *When health is absent, wisdom cannot*
> *reveal itself, or cannot manifest, strength*
> *cannot fight, wealth becomes useless and*
> *intelligence cannot be applied. –*
> *Herophilus*

Spiritual Crisis

Spiritual crisis causes great stress on the individual, as well as being a contributing factor in physical and mental health problems. Depending on your religious convictions, many have questioned why God allowed this to happen. One might question if there is a Loving God, how could He allow this to happen at all, or why would God want to will this trauma on anyone. We have all been given the agency to choose right or wrong, and in some of the wrong choices it affects individuals not responsible for that wrongness. In the scriptures, it is written over and over to put your pains and fears into the Lord's hands, and He will carry the burden for you. His sacrifice was sufficient for us all. He understands and knows how to heal our pains so turn your hearts to Him. The Lord never willed anyone to experience sexual abuse so that they could learn some lesson from it; that is not His will. However, if Divine intervention happened every time an innocent person was going to be a victim, then there would be no reason for choices. Our agency would be removed, and that is also not His plan. He knows what is in our hearts and understands the evil acts of man. Abuse is always wrong and fervently condemned by the Lord.

It were better for him that a millstone
were hanged about his neck, and he cast
into the sea, than that he should offend
one of these little ones. – Luke 17:2

Many people see sexual assault as a victim's sin, that if the survivor did not fight as much as possible, they have committed a sin. Others place so much on the physical virginity of women, they forget virtuous goes along in line with it. A woman who's a virgin and that is taken from her still holds her virtuousness. Just as a person who is victim of a murder is not held to a mythical sin of being a murdered victim. You are not held accountable for the sins others commit. Some religions condemn the victim. I do know a loving God does not condemn someone for what has happened to them.

I, the Lord, will forgive whom I will
forgive, but of you it is required to forgive
all men. D&C 64:10

Forgiveness
Forgiveness is a subject many people do not thoroughly comprehend. Forgiveness does not suggest you are denying your feelings by avoiding the issue. It is also Not condoning the act, by not seeking legal justice (filing a report, going through with the trial with the purpose of trying to stop him from assaulting anyone else). Holding another person accountable for actions in which they have committed through the laws, has absolutely nothing to do with forgiveness. Just as continuing any relationship with that person, no matter who they are. Once a person has been forgiven, it does not

wipe the slate clean to allow any further abuse. You could have already forgiven the perpetrator and still go forward with legal actions to have that person held accountable for what has been done. Forgiveness is letting go of the hate and revengeful thoughts and trusting in the Lord that no matter the earthly outcome, justice, true justice will always prevail in the eternal end.

In a book I read, it touched on the issue of forgiveness writing "This is a request to (1) pardon the transgression, (2) release the anger and hurt, and (3) mend a relationship" (Katz, 2015). As I stated, giving forgiveness is not a request for any of what was written. If that is what is being asked, that is not forgiveness. I also completely disagree with the author's statement of "The fact is some acts are unforgivable." This is incorrect. It states in the Bible, forgive all......forgiveness is between you and God. It does not have to include the perp, in that he is let off the hook, allowed any access to you, and/or mend any real or perceived relationship. Forgiveness is not forgetness. Forgiveness is not relinquishing that person's sin from accountability and civil justice.

Real forgiveness goes in line with justice, Supreme, Divine justice, not some - maybe, some day, they could get theirs. No, there is a final judgment. That perp will be judged for what he did. He's not going to be able to hire some lawyer to play on words or use excuses to get off. Let me be very direct. Forgiveness from the victim to the perp is not the same road as forgiveness from the perp to the victim. There is much more involved for the one who committed the wrong, than the one who the wrong was committed on. With the perp, it is not the releasing of hate and vengeful thoughts. Their process, and it is a process, comes at great exertion. It is not some passive, "I'm sorry, please forgive me." No, if they truly are seeking real forgiveness, it starts with acknowledging what they did was their choice. It was evil. Confess to proper authority (religious as well as legal); accept whatever punishment is required;

plead guilty – no deals, no bargaining, no excuses; feel culpable and shameful for what they did; accept the victim rights and wishes (if you do not want to see him, or respond to, or whatever you feel); contemplate upon the vicious sin; after severe lamentation, ask for the Lord's forgiveness; continue to respect the victim's rights and wishes; and take whatever action is warranted to never perpetrate this nefarious sin upon anyone again, for the rest of their life.

When you forgive, you heal your own anger and hurt and are able to let love lead again. It's like spring cleaning for your heart. – Marci Shimoff

---

Stress

Stress has been linked with an array of medical problems, both physical and mental. There is considered good stress, and bad stress, the deviation is our perception, but both still have chemical effects on our bodies. A positive stressor could be a wedding, and just as easily, it also can be tossed into the negative side. The chemicals released by a good or bad stress doesn't necessarily react differently on the physical body.

Think of a normal day, how many stressful concerns do you have? Work? Kids? Finances? I could just say, well it's just perception, what is seen as an emergency today, will be just another thing tomorrow, but I know it isn't that simple. I've tried all sorts of unprecedented systems to rank what really warrants my attention and what can be put off or isn't as important, and came up with my own. It works for me, but figuring out your own system can take a little while. Placing items on ranking list really helped. Nevertheless, even more than that was taking the eternal perspective and applying it to everything. When you know your mission in this life, questioning whether or not something deserves the energy of your attention you're giving it, becomes much easier.

During stressful situations you can seemly react with more singularity to focus. Your brain gets more oxygen; you release hormones; increased heart rate; increased breathing rate. And for short bits of time, it is healthy. But if we looked at everything as though it was an emergency, our life, more likely than not, would be shortened and riddled with medical problems. It is a problem when you're late for work; however, what good is it to start that downward spiral of the Ants?

All this stress starts to continually disrupt your mind with never ending worries which can cause anxiety. Worrying about what's going to happen, if you'll get fired? How you'll make next week's payment? Where will you find this type of work, and on and on? But what does all this worrying do? Will it get you to work faster? No. Will it help you make next week's payments? No. Get you another job? No. What does worrying do? The studies I investigated persistently, show all this stress can cause a myriad of physical and mental illnesses, not just minor concerns but actual serious illnesses. Anxiety, high blood pressure; heart attack; insomnia; heartburn; rapid breathing; headaches; depression; irritability; irregular menstrual cycle; stomach ache; back ache, and the list goes on and on.

Having your life plan helps. It can prepare you for what is coming ahead and allow you time to ponder and possibly come up with different decisions. The eternal perspective does give many of what used to be emergency stressful situations, a dose of eternal reality. It is not going to completely remove stress from your life, but I promise you it will significantly help. And when those surprise stressful times happen, go to your backpack, get your plan, start using your new coping skills, pull out your support symptom list and ask for help; breathe and especially pray.

> *Come unto me, all ye that labour and*
> *are heavy laden, and I will give you rest. –*
> *Matt. 11:28*

Substance Use & Abuse

Just as with depression, your abuse of a substance can be considered a mental diagnosis all on its own - Substance Use/Abuse Disorder. What is substance use and abuse? When the majority hear the term substance abuse, they think primarily alcohol and illicit drugs (cocaine, heroin, marijuana, etc.), but the word 'substance' actually identities any physical matter. In the case of mental health issues it chiefly relates to substances we take into the body. In the DSM-V, the listed disorders are: alcohol, caffeine, cannabis, hallucinogens (phencyclidine, other hallucinogens) inhalants, opioids, sedatives (hypnotics or anxiolytic), stimulants, tobacco, and other (or unknown). Every substance listed is a diagnosis for a use disorder except caffeine, it is under Caffeine Intoxication. Other or Unknown substances is a catch-all for anything else taken into the body and satisfies the qualifications.

"The essential feature of a substance use is a cluster of cognitive, behavioral and physiological symptoms indicating that the individual continues using the substance despite significant substance-related problems. An important characteristic of substance use disorders is an underlying change in brain circuits that may persist beyond detoxification, particularly in individuals with severe disorders. The behavioral effects of these brain changes may be exhibited in the repeated relapses and intense drug craving when the individuals are exposed to drug-related stimuli" (DSM-V, 2013).

There are four common indications for substance use (ab)use: impaired control; social impairment; risky use; and pharmacological. When you take larger amounts of the substance or take it for longer than it was initially intended your control is impaired. The intake may result in not being able to perform at work, school, home, and/or any other significant role obligations. Along with that, in your interpersonal or close group, it causes problems, signifying a social impairment. Your ab(use) of the substance is under circumstances where it is physically dangerous; and you continue (ab)using even though it is causing psychological or physical problems. Your required increase (ab)use to gain the same desired effect is a criterion for pharmacological. It also includes withdrawal symptoms not due to medical treatment.

There is a high correlation between a diagnosis of PTSD from experiencing a MST and co-occurring (dual diagnosis) disorder of Substance (Ab)use. One theory behind this is the survivor is attempting to self-medicate because of the PTSD symptoms. (Ab)uses of these substances can mask, or decrease some of the PTSD symptoms; however, you are not dealing with the underlined problem but adding on other non-PTSD woes. In the past, professionals, as well as organizations have directed their attention to the treatment of one or the other. Some may facilitate sufferers of PTSD, as long as they currently are not (ab)using; or after they've been through a substance (ab)use program. The research behind fixating on one or the other verified a drastic opt-out of treatment from the victim, in essence for most, if both are not concurrently treated, it just does not effectively work.

Even without possessing the full criteria to be diagnosed with a substance (ab)use disorder, this does not constitute that you do not possess an ab(use) problem. Anytime you must have additional substances not medically relevant, this generates a problem. Let's take alcohol. If you need a glass of alcohol (beer, wine, whiskey) to:

relax; become more fun; sleep; decompress and/or any other reason to augment your system, you have a problem. If a feeling becomes overwhelming and you suppress it with alcohol, you have a problem. In the beginning, it may not interfere with your functioning; however, it is a disaster waiting to happen.

Now, and this one will vex a lot of you. Do you require a cup of coffee (or more) to: wake up, think straight, and/or function? Then you also have a problem. You essentially are drugging yourself – caffeine (possibly also your sugar content) to make your body perform its normal functions. You have altered your perception and body to need this drug. What would happen if you had no caffeine tomorrow? Would you become agitated, maybe shake, get a headache (or migraine), forget things – essentially go into withdrawals? Most say that there are many things which contain caffeine, but you would die from a sugar coma before getting close to the same intake.

If you have been diagnosed with a substance disorder I would eliminate all of the stated substances completely, as well as any other substances, which you seem drawn to, or taken when you're experiencing a PTSD, MMD, or Anxiety symptom, that is not medically prescribed by a psychiatrist.

I can do all things through Christ
which strengtheneth me. – Phil 4:13

Other Illnesses

It has been a relentless annoyance to remind doctors and especially ones in the mental health sector, that I am not my mental health diagnosis; that I'm seeing them for. I am a whole person that comes with other physical and mental health burdens. My other infirmities can become secondary, when the pain of the migraine trumps all; secondary but did not vanish. I also have been with my body all my life and am pretty sure I know it better than the doctors. No, I did not go to medical school, but it doesn't require a degree to explain the symptoms. Sometimes I have no choice but to spell out the side effects the meds give me – even if they are not on the official side-effect list, and the doctor has never heard that happening before. I also am tired of being a VA guinea pig, so I've taken my health decisions completely back.

Yes, I have a clinical diagnosis of PTSD; however, all the symptoms are not totally known to be just from PTSD. And it's an irritant to remind therapists that the symptoms I'm having, may not be ones that can or necessitate being worked through. I have some that are from other injuries, and it is not a matter of saying some positive praise or going back to my childhood to uncover the origin. I know what it was and it's not a part of my mental health, per se. Mental diagnoses have so many cross over of symptoms, you can have some or many of them that could be attributed to a specific diagnosis, maybe not. I have headaches; cluster, tension and because of taking the medication, rebound headaches. I also get migraines, which are different than headaches. I have memory loss, confusion, irritability, sleep problems, jumpiness, and the list goes on, but they are not all attributed to only PTSD. I have had multiple head injuries which caused loss of consciousness. I was in the Gulf War and exposed to some nasty chemicals; that the government will not acknowledge or identify. I am getting older and going through 'woman changes.' So when I am seeing a counselor for symptoms from other illnesses, it is not a symptom of PTSD; so stop placing everything into that box. My brain and body do not work like they used to, and many times it uniquely responds medically-mysterious.

As I juxtapose my medical health checklist from going into the military and the one leaving it, it's a huge discrepancy. It doesn't seem they could possibility be from the same person. Going in I had about two 'yes'es' from medical injuries/problems. I'd had an ear infection which eventually ruptured my eardrum, and a dog bite on my right upper arm, which had required a trip to the ER and stitches. That's it. I'd never had the mumps or measles or chicken poxes. I never had a headache, let alone a migraine prior to enlistment. No broken bones, two ER trips (for what was listed above). No other doctor appointments of any magnitude. I can only remember getting sick twice, and it was because of what I ate. Oh, I played the sick game to get out of school, but my mom pretty much knew I just didn't want to go. When I departed the military, there were all sorts of checkmarks. It definitely did not appear to be the same person with only 4 years between them, but that's how it is.

I have other maladies which demand constant medical care. At times it can be a full-time job. When a migraine comes and I'm down for at least the rest of that day, my other aliments don't take a break. I have good days, bad days and then skip days, skipped because I am not functionable at all.

Just as I am not my mental health disorder; I'm also not my physical health disabilities. I am all of that and still a person who will have a purposeful life. So I have had to become a researcher in my ailments; looking up symptoms and 'cures.' I am not about to medicate myself back to zombie as the VA most definitely seems to want me there. I also have had to become very assertive toward many VA doctors. And try my own researched therapies – vitamins, yoga, writing, substance control. It has been a long lonely road, until the internet, and that has been a lifesaver. I can communicate with others who have similar problems, from their military experiences, and adjust my routine when needed.

So what other illnesses do you have? Which of them have the same symptoms that could be attributed to a different mental health illness? Can you get close to when they started to occur and attach them to another injury?

So what other aliments do you have? Are you putting them completely aside and focusing only on certain ones? Why?

Your mind, emotions and body are instruments and the way you align and tune them determines how well you play life. – Yogi Bhajan

---

7
THERAPY

Mental Illness

All emotions, feelings, and thoughts are on a ranged-spectrum of normality to clinically diagnosable. Most people can interconnect the terms used for symptoms of mental illness and their own perceptions. We've all have been sad, even exceedingly sad, and been happy, even ecstatic. But bipolar (manic depressive) disorder moves your gauge from one end of the continuum – depression; to the other - (manic), within that person's own set roller coaster. It could be from one side to the other side in hours, days, or weeks, and staying in each red zone is also as individual and erratic.

Many people fear the diagnosis of a mental disorder. Social stigma has a negative portrayal of mentally disturbed villains who can or do notorious atrocities towards others, consistently making us cringe even thinking about it, but these are scarce. Even though most people with mental disorders are not violent, or out of touch with reality; there is a stereotypical belief they could lose control at any time and end up killing the ones they love. Not to mention hurting other innocent people.

When a person commits an unspeakable crime, and they had been in the military, the media purposely uses the picture of them in their uniform, no matter how long ago it was, when talking about the crime. It is deliberate to popularize the myth that all veterans are prone to violence and especially if the veteran can be associated with some conflict or war; whether they deployed or not. This deeply adds to the stigma that something went mentally wrong with these people whose jobs were to protect our country. It also falls into my conspiracy theorist friend's ideology, that there are people in power (who dominate the media) injecting in the mind of the average citizen that veterans, especially ones who have been in hot zones, are mentally unstable, and eventually their rights to own firearms will be taken away to protect the public. The first thing in controlling a country is to disarm them, and who better to start disarming than ones trained to use them?

Just because an individual executes some heinous act does not automatically determine that they have a mental illness. Many sane people commit horrific evils. Unfortunately, many of these evils were wrongly attributed to a mental illness, because it is hard for most to think evil deeds are purposely done by someone who is lucid; but that is the reality. In an attempt to explain away the evil act, most want to have answers outside of choice, which caused something mentally to go wrong, to explain other than the truth. That truth is the assailants have thoughtfully chosen to do evil.

A new reinforcement in stereotyping mentally ill persons, is the use of psychological terminology and mental health diagnoses, by person who toss these terms out without any education behind them. These (Facebook) psychologist read some posting and instead of actually doing any investigation, they believe what has been posted. Quickly responding with another post with the same asinine information. Words that are mental-health based are becoming popular buzz words, losing all their original meaning.

So, surfing on the internet, inside many social chatting sites, you come across many people attributing a mental health disorder to a character flaw or idiosyncrasy (quirk, oddity) of theirs. I come across it all the time, someone saying their OCD was acting up, or their OCD is coming out. At times I just go on with the next posting, but then there are the other times where I just cannot seem to let it go. Having a mental disorder is not some minor inconvenience and the majority needs to be informed about this. Talking about having to have the eggs in your egg carton on the left side, or right, or whatever, is not automatically OCD, it can and usually is what you prefer. Just as with the pens on your desk or how spoons must all be up stacked one on the other in the drawer. OCD is not that simple.

OCD –

The characteristic symptoms of OCD are the presence of obsessions and compulsions. Obsessions are repetitive and persistent thoughts, images, or urges. Importantly, obsessions are not pleasurable or experienced as voluntary: they are intrusive and unwanted and cause marked distress or anxiety in most individuals. The individual attempts to ignore or suppress these obsessions or to neutralize them with another thought or action. Compulsions are repetitive behaviors or mental acts that the individual feels driven to perform in response to an obsession or according to rules that must be applied rigidly. Most individuals with OCD have both obsessions and compulsions. The aim is to reduce the distress triggered by obsessions or to prevent a feared event. However, these compulsions either are not connected in a realistic way to the feared event or are clearly excessive. Compulsions are not done for pleasure, although some individuals experience relief from anxiety or distress. The obsessions and compulsions must be time-consuming (e.g., more than 1 hour per day) or cause clinically significant distress or impairment to warrant a diagnosis of OCD (DSM-V, 2013).

There are some other criteria for OCD which limits it to not another disorder, but just from the criteria above, commenting on some quirk of yours, a pet peeve, or some other part of your preferences as OCD, lessens what it is really like to truly have this disorder and perpetuates widespread misunderstanding. I used OCD as an example, but it expands to all mental health disorders. Tossing the words around for anything less than what they truly are, increases the fallacy for mental illnesses and executes a formidable injustice to all.

Diagnosis

Once a person has been diagnosed with a mental disorder, it is advantageous to research the particular disorder, comprehending the criteria, and learn the reasons behind the decision. Read the DSM-V listing of your diagnosed disorder. Do not rely on pamphlets, rumors and especially not keyboard shrinks to deliver a comprehensive representation. I would print it off to occasionally look over it and have it handy in case you come across someone posting something that just doesn't ring factual, and maybe pleasantly enlighten them. Ask your therapist to expound their rational for ascribing that individual disorder. This is not an attempt to question the diagnosis, or the therapist, but enhance the patient's ability to assist in their own therapeutic journey.

Reading through the criteria of disorders in the DSM-V, countless MST survivors find their symptoms mirrored on many pages; however, one very relevant criterion is the trauma itself. If the altering point of your "then" reactions (feeling normal) to the "current" ones (uncharacteristic of who you were) is the traumatic event, then PTSD seems to be the best diagnosis for MST survivors whose symptoms are within the specific criteria. Another contributing factor for an appropriate mental health diagnosis is patient disclosure. Most have trust issues, and disclosing of information, even valuable information necessary for a competent diagnosis can come sluggishly and with difficulty, causing multiple diagnoses and even misdiagnosis.

The term comorbidity refers to having more than one disorder. Because a person has been diagnosed with one mental disorder, does not preclude all others, as numerous people can have more than one diagnosed mental disorder. Once a symptom attains the criteria for another mental disorder on its own – you have comorbidity, co-occurring disorders. Comorbidity can prompt one evaluator to affirm one diagnosis while another evaluator bestows another. This dual (or more) diagnosis does not constitute a misdiagnosis, but reveals the complexity of a person's potential life experiences, and possible genetic mental maladjustments.

An infuriation of mine is using the term military sexual trauma as if it is some disease or diagnosis. Recently I read off a posting "My MST is acting up." I desired to put, "No, your ignorance is" but I did not. Even diagnosed with PTSD, it is not 'coming out' or 'acting up.' Mental health diagnosed disorder are a cluster of symptoms, not one, as in having a symptom or virus. Since only some of the listed criteria is essential for a diagnosis, saying your PTSD is acting up, says essentially nothing. Is it the hypervigilance? Avoidance? Memories? Flashback? Nightmares? And it does not resolve that all the symptoms you have are at the same levels of intensity.

I grasp the confusion of the term, especially when the VA has an ever changing definition on its site, hinging on what page you click. Military sexual trauma is an experience. Just as I do not have rape and I do not have combat, I do not have MST. When applying for disability, identify the diagnosis (which MST is not); the cluster of symptoms which all together fulfill the criteria for a mental health diagnosis, which you currently suffer from, by experiencing a MST. MST is never what you have been given a disability rating for, if it was, anyone who experienced MST would be considered service-connected.

Posttraumatic Stress Disorder
There is evidence that military sexual assault makes PTSD more likely than a similar assault before or after military service, and increases the likelihood of developing PTSD (Committee on Treatment of Posttraumatic Stress Disorder, 2007).

Diagnostic criteria for PTSD include a history of exposure to a traumatic event that meets specific stipulations and symptoms from each of the four symptoms clusters: intrusion, avoidance, negative alterations in cognitions and mood, and alterations in arousal and reactivity. The sixth criterion concerns duration of symptoms; the seventh assesses functioning and the eighth criterion clarifies symptoms as not attributed to a substance or co-occurring medical condition (ptsd.va.gov, 2016).

Some of the symptoms for the diagnosed criteria:
- Intrusive distressing memories
- Flashbacks
- Avoidance (of places and thinking about the trauma)
- Emotional numbing
- Lack of interest
- Memory problems
- Irritability
- Negative feelings about self, people
- Inability to feel positive feelings
- Hypervigilance
- Sleep problems
- Risky behaviors

Another diagnosis routinely given to survivors of MST is - Major Depressive Disorder. Major Depressive Disorder is the check off of at least five or more of: a depressed mood; loss of interest or pleasure; weight loss or gain by 5%; insomnia or hypersomnia; psychomotor agitation; loss of energy or fatigue; worthless feeling or excessive inappropriate guilt; inability to concentrate, indecisive and or recurrent thoughts of death (not just afraid of dying); suicidal ideation, with our without a specific plan, and an attempt of suicide. Beside the weight change and thoughts of death (including suicide) to be considered a criterion they must have occurred nearly everyday, for most of the day, are a change from the persons previous mood and occur during the same two week period" (DSM-V, 2013).

> *You treat a disease, you win, you lose.*
> *You treat a person, I guarantee you, you'll*
> *win, no matter what the outcome. – Robin*
> *Williams*

Organizations, Programs, and Groups

I have researched, been a member of, critiqued, consulted, wrote and been a participant of many different types of organizations, programs, and groups; from VA, in profit, in non-profit, and in private settings. There were some good ones. Ones that the people putting them on had good intentions, just did not grasp what they were doing. And others that I cannot really tell if they purposely wanted to add to the trauma or were just that clueless. When looking at being involved (as a volunteer, giving money, being a participant, or working for) with any type of organization, program or group, research it, know what you are getting into.

I learned quite a lot looking into and volunteering for many organizations. At first I tried to be what they thought they needed. I tried to be helpful and got the "no thanks," from many. It amazed me how many people were so very threatened by my volunteering. I laugh when I went into the profit side, it was completely different; they wanted anything that I was willing to help with. There wasn't the jealousy, the back stabbing, the sabotaging, bad talking of another organizations and the ultimate – the "mine" mentality. Many non-profits don't like or want to share – anything. As my husband says "they don't play well in the sand box."

As previously stated, you can be 'healed' from PTSD, but that in no way suggests you are symptom free. Healed only indicates you no longer have all the criteria for a diagnosis. Beware of programs which announce they can 'cure' you from all mental illnesses, or a specifically named disorder in 5, 10, 15 easy sessions, or such. There are many supportive organizations, programs and groups, but it is essential to know which ones will be helpful for you. I personally and professionally do not like any program which has a survivor detail their experience in a group setting. Hearing the details about any trauma can trigger you. Going over the details of your own trauma, will continually etch it into your mind and body. Talking about feelings and responses you are having now, is very different, but even that can be triggering.

Ask yourself what you presuppose you will get out of participating? Ask questions about anything you do not understand and do not feel kooky, this is your journey. I have come across programs which say they are for MST survivors but when further investigating, the program was either written generally to help out with trauma or another specific trauma, but not MST. Some organizations do not understand the programs they run and unfortunately there are more than you think. They take other programs meant for another trauma and think all PTSD is the same. This happens a lot with programs designed for veterans. They are written to help combat veterans and the organization just adds MST to the pamphlet, thinking it's all the same, and it is not.

Some organizations take programs for sexual assaults and declare they are specifically to help with the aftermaths of MST. But MST is a unique type of sexual cruelty, and all programs for sexual assaults also are not all the same. Only a program written specifically with the unique traits, most MST survivors have endured, is explicitly for MST survivors. Other programs can be helpful, but most omitted some distinctive aspects related to suffering a MST. If the people running the program do not discern there is a difference, they are typically using a program they had no input in developing, and have no reason to be employing.

I am cautious about programs which ask you to change too much all at once. I was in such a program and although the ones who were in control, had good intentions, they missed out of what a truly exquisite program includes – the whole self. Therapists sometimes forget they are not medical doctors. They are so targeted on the mental side of health, they forget the physical side of health. The program had not taken into account what withdrawals from sugar, caffeine and processed foods can do to a body. They understood healthy food is best, but it should have been listed in the program description, withdrawals are not amusing, and can hamper your energy to work on other issues.

When a program is conducted away from your home, where you must stay at, or in a nearby hotel, ask about the meals and availability of other foods. As I said I was in such a program. I was not the only person who had withdrawal symptoms because of immediate dietary changes. It is not healthy to do that to a body. And to top it all off it was an intense program for trauma. I watched as others missed out on group, did not participate fully, and/or spaced out; all because of the drastic changes we were put through. Do not feel embarrassed when questioning about the conditions of the facilities, meals, activities, and restrictions. And if you want to educate them on any of those items, do it, I have. It is much better to figure out that just is not going to work for you (ever or at this time) than be surprised and go through uncomfortable, stressful times, which can seriously trigger or hurt your health. Don't be the guinea pig.

Open drop in groups, may be a little frustrating when you have trust issues. These groups allow any person who meets the target criteria to come when they want. It takes a while in a new group to begin to put trust in the other members. Some groups which have confidentially agreements might seem a bit safer; however, just because someone agrees to keep everything in the group as confidential, does not promise that they will honor that agreement. That is why drop-in groups can seem to revert backwards, when a new member joins. Although the group has formed a certain amount of trust with one another, the new member can cause what had been a trusted discussion to turn into a censored one.

The programs and groups which I feel utilize time and resources best (for them and me) is psychoeducational groups. As in most the groups, I attend, I go for myself. When I go, I am Miette Wells, participant. If it is a training or I've been asked to critique the program/group, then I am Dr. Wells. It is not hard for me to separate that. What is difficult is attending as a participant and watching the program not be followed, not be utilized for the appropriate and/or (this one drives me crazy) have the staff or another participant say something incorrect and when I try and correct it, the facilitator says, "That is what is in the guide." Understand the "guide" not only is not all knowing, many of them are actually incorrect, and/or completely outdated. Eventually, I am going to just say, "Allow me to introduce myself – I'm Dr. Wells." It is exasperating that only when I toss the Dr. on do I get listened to, as if the only way you have any knowledge is with a degree. That is utterly untrue, but sometimes it is all they are willing to listen to, which is very disheartening.

I am very guarded with who I am in addition to just as a participant, but there are so many times I get students who happen to be studying psychology, say something totally inaccurate, and I just cannot let it go. I have found more people, and especially staff, of these organizations, who really do not know what they are talking about, are the ones talking the most. They have taken the 2 plus hour course and now are thinking they are experts in the field. I do not know everything about all mental illnesses, not even everything about one, but I do know quite a lot about the specific ones I write about, as well as issued surrounding women veterans, and MST survivors.

A good group is one where the facilitator has been educated beyond the guides. They do not have to have a degree. They however, should be required to understand the major apprehensions the survivors will be discussing. I love homework, handouts and fill-ins. It doesn't matter if the homework doesn't get done by everyone, or blanks are left in the fill-in and/or the handouts are folded into air planes. There are enough people who truly have the desire to want to help themselves and are starving for this information. They just hunger for a gentle hand to guide them. Whole workbooks are great, and I don't mind, if it is a numbered session group, that they are left at the facility, but additional handouts should be included. Three ring binder notebooks are favored because you can be given homework by removing the pages, then put them back in at the next meeting. At the end, you have this wealth of information that's been personalized to you. But again question before heading into any of these groups or programs.

Therapists

Establishing a relationship of trust with the therapist can lead to restructuring significant emotional experiences. Therefore, the relationship you establish with your therapist is the basic foundation for therapy. This relationship is crucial to working through the underlined causes and hopefully resulting in the lessening of symptoms, eliminations of symptoms and bringing functionability back into your life. Choosing a therapist and the modality of therapy is not as easy as it might first seem. The specialized techniques utilized by psychotherapy can cause lasting changes in your life, even if they are exhibiting acute, short-term problems. The credentialing of therapists is exceedingly confusing; there are hundreds of designations and someone can instantly feel as though they are in alphabet soup (L.C.S.W., L.P.C., M.D., DPsy, to name a few). Not all therapists or counselors prescribe to the same types of therapy. There is a tremendously significant difference in the various therapies, as well as the way different therapists practice the same modality.

Have you ever just met someone and knew you would be great friends or that you just do not click? These unconscious messages are real and should be listened to. They are communications from you to yourself. When you look for a therapist, learn how to utilize these unconscious messages to your advantage, because they can be tricky. Many times your conscious and unconscious mind seem to contradict one another. Using these unconscious pieces of information, through feelings, responses and also sometimes dreams, to evaluate the connectedness you have with a therapist and their therapy, is essential. Do not ignore your gut reactions, apply them in helping to choose the right therapist and therapy. This is your therapy, not the therapist's.

Privacy is an essential aspect of therapy. Everyone has a right to complete privacy during sessions, as well as absolute confidentiality. Nobody should be able to listen in on therapeutic sessions, directly or indirectly. The therapist should not be discussing any aspect of the sessions with anyone else, without written authorization from all participants; unless there is legal responsibility for the therapist to do so. All information should stay in confidential files unless authorized otherwise, and you should know what information will be shared, with and without permission.

You do not have to accept the therapist the VA has. Until recently, there has only been male social workers for my VA therapy, so I told the VA that is just is not going to work out for me. I had an outside counselor, female, which the VA payed for. There were a few hoops to jump through but it can be done, and it is much easier to do now than when I first started using the VA.

I have been pushed by "professionals" to try some new technique. One such technique was EMDR. I do know there are many this helps. There are also many therapist who use it and really should not be. They are not experienced enough and some take a simple weekend course and believe they now have mastered its application. I actually ask any therapist, who wants to try something new, how long they have been doing it, where they learned it from and research their answers before either agreeing or passing on, all new techniques. The therapist who first tried EMDR on me was very skilled. Unfortunately, because of my head injury, the moving of the eyes like that creates headaches which completely detract from what we are working on. I also cannot do the tapping, on any part of my body or tones in any rhythmic sequence, total irritation leading to headaches. Years later, I had another therapist question about trying it. I related it did not work on me and caused pain. But she "knew" that it just had not had been done right. I was pushed into accepting to try again. This time it was not just a headache which demanded medication and rest, it was a full blown migraine and serious knockout drugs.

There are certain items to keep in mind when selecting a therapist. Make sure you are not pushed into selecting a particular therapist by anyone, friend, family member or another healthcare provider. The therapist should not be seeing someone which you are friends with or good acquaintances. The therapist should not be related to you, or a friend, the relative of a friend, or even the friend of a friend. In selecting, remove any person who can be connected in any way other than as a therapist.

> *Our sorrows and wounds are healed*
> *only when we touch them with*
> *compassion. – Buddha*

Therapies

Therapy:

1. The treatment of disease or disorders, as by some remedial, rehabilitating, or curative process: speech therapy.
2. A curative power or quality.
3. Psychotherapy.
4. Any act, hobby, task, program, etc., that relieves tension (dictionary.com, 2016).

No two people are the same, just as no two sexual assaults, even if the victim or perpetrator are the same; therefore, it is absurd to believe all military sexual trauma victims will benefit from just one modality of therapy. One way to determine which therapy could help to reduce negative symptoms and be able to positively cope with automatic reactions, is to create a list of ten, investigate what each entails and eliminate ones you have absolutely no faith in or seem wacked. Make a list of the possibilities combined with the ones not dejected and you have a sincere beginning at which to start. Understand most therapist employ more than one type of therapy, just as you can select more than one. There are numerous positive elements associated with the diversity of therapies, which hopefully will help in the healing process.

If you are a veteran, VA provides free confidential counseling and treatment for physical and mental conditions related to MST experiences. A veteran does not need to be service connected, and may be able to receive the counseling and treatment even if they otherwise are not eligible for other VA care. Evidence of, reporting of the incident(s), or military documenting the trauma occurred, is not necessary. If you are already seeking medical care at a VA facility, speak to your primary health care provider (va.gov, 2015).

There is supposed to be a designated MST Coordinator at every VA facility and a contact person for all MST-related issues. This coordinator is the advocate for finding and accessing community resources, state and federal benefits, and VA services and programs.

Military Sexual Trauma is determined by the statement of the veteran declaring they experienced MST. Eligibility for services is determined by the VA clinician, who determines which problems are related to the MST, other than therapy. It can be seen as admirable that the VA allows the receiving of free counseling and/or medical care for problems associated with experiencing MST; however, a medical clinician will establish what is and is not linked. Nobody can totally determine to an exact point what physical and mental conditions do and do not relate to MST. Because of such, it is advantageous to proceed to a disability claim when the symptoms of experiencing MST interrupt your daily life.

Psychotherapy - the treatment of psychological disorders or maladjustments by a professional technique, as psychoanalysis, group therapy, or behavioral therapy (dictionary.com, 2016).

Cognitive Behavior Therapy (CBT) generally seeks to identify harmful thought(s) and thought patterns with the intent of changing/influencing destructive pessimistic emotions and dysfunctional behaviors. It is a collaborative effort between the therapist and client; the therapist listens then encouragingly teaches the client ways in which to unlearn the maladaptive emotions and behaviors. CBT is based on the idea that our thoughts cause our feelings and behaviors, not external conditions, and that we can change the way we think/feel even if the situation does not change. CBT is said (generally) to be the most rapid in terms of results, with a time-limit (session limited) process, highly instructive and giving the client homework.

Dialectical Behavioral Therapy (DBT) mainly utilized for Borderline Personality Disorders, is interested in: first, reducing self-injuring and self-threatening behaviors; then reducing behaviors which interfere with the therapy process; eventually decreasing behaviors that diminish the client's quality of life.

Rational Emotive Behavior Therapy (REBT) views people as prone to embracing irrational beliefs and behaviors, which stand in the way of them accomplishing their purposes and goals. These irrational attitudes take on extreme positions that contrast to healthy rational and flexible wants and desires of the person. The primary focus is on the present and not past trauma(s), and that we do not have to allow the past to influence the way we view the present.

Stress Inoculation Training has three components to the method: education, skill building and application. SIT is an anxiety management treatment therapy utilized generally to treat fear and anxiety symptoms. SIT is also a time-limited therapy with usually 10-14 sessions where the therapist will educate the client on: identifying cues in the environment which trigger responses; how fear develops as a learned response to trauma; and relaxation exercises. In the skills building segment, the therapist helps the client learn how to control their emotional reactions, and is intended to reduce negative thoughts and physiological sensations. The client then applies the skills learned in managing their response to stimuli and their anxiety symptoms.

Prolonged Exposure Therapy (PET) is based on the concept that we can get used to things that are just annoying and not truly life-threatening or dangerous. With PET, the therapist asks the client to confront the very situations, people, memories, and objects which are attached to the trauma, but conducted in a safe method. It can be done with in vivo (real life), like going to the local park where the trauma occurred, or is associated with imagining you are in the park. PET deems that avoidance of the discomfort reinforces avoidance as a coping skill, and increases the likelihood the anxiety might spread to other aspects of the person's life. Continuation of the exposure is essential to reducing the frequency and severity of the symptoms. This form of therapy can be very emotionally painful for survivors and is not used for every client.

Pharmacotherapy. The symptoms from experiencing MST can become so debilitating that psychotherapy cannot adequately begin without pharmacotherapy (medication). Taking medications is not pathetic. For certain intense symptoms, it is necessary. These medications need not be thought of as a cure-all but as a helper to reduce the issues standing in the way of psychotherapy. Even though a medication is proposed, do not just take it without consideration of the possible benefits and possible harm (side effects) it can do. The benefits to accepting the medication can be: fast working; treat coexisting disorders; stop the escalation of a crisis situation; and (but not limited to) allow you to function until the next therapeutic session. Some of the dilemmas to accepting these medications are: some cause serious medical side effects; dependency on the medication; lead to a denial there is something wrong; causing more symptoms; and sometimes they just do not work (causing more anxiety). Understanding all the implications to taking a prescribed medication is in your best interest. Sometimes the side effects of the medications are worse than the symptoms you are taking them for and will likely focus on just one symptom.

Acupressure is the process of using finger pressure on specific points on the body.

Acupuncture is the process of using needles (small fine needles), which are inserted at specific points on the body to restore a vital energy balance.

Aromatherapy is the utilization of essential oils, which can be, massaged into the skin, inhaled or added to water (baths, soaking of a specific part of the body), commonly in a diluted manner.

Bibliotherapy uses the connection the client has with selected written works (books, poems, papers) to assist in solving problems and is often combined with writing therapy. Within the context of the written work, the individual can: see themselves; relate to the experience; discover personal negative behaviors; connect with any of the characters; experience emotional happiness. All with the understanding that it will be a positive in the client's life.

Biofeedback employs the use of machinery to monitor the individual's metabolic system, having the ability in real time to view the changes and modify them to a poised internal state. The client learns to recognize when their system is negatively responding to a word, memory, picture, etc., and then with the assistance of the therapist, can alter them accordingly.

Emotional Freedom Technique (Tapping Therapy) is a subset of Meridian Tapping Technique. In describing it in its simplest form, it is tapping on certain acupressure points while focusing on a behavior, feeling and/or thought, and that negative feeling, thought and/or behavior is allowed to flow beyond its stuck points.

Eye Movement Desensitization and Reprocessing (EMDR) contains many aspects of different modalities: interpersonal, cognitive behavioral, psychodynamic and body-centered. In the process, the therapist asks the client to focus on a thought or picture (in the mind), then uses an apparatus (finger, pen, light dot) to have the patient follow with their eyes back and forth. After an amount of time, the eye movement is halted and the therapist inquires as to what thoughts, visions etc. has come up. Investigation into that feeling, thought, memory, etc. proceeds or can be the focus and the eye movement begins again. The element used is dual stimulation: bilateral eye movements and tones or taps while the client attends to memories, present triggers, or future experiences. The client begins to replace the negative beliefs with positive ones (which were discussed previous to the session). The duality initiates the emergence of insight, new associations and/or changes in memories. The process is repeated several times while the therapist allows the client to work through their own stuck issues.

Herbalism employs the use of plants or plant-based substances to aid in whatever ailment the person is having.

Homoeopathy is a medical system which draws on the theory that like treats like. A remedy is a minute diluted dose of a natural substance (sometime diluted to the extreme), which if taken in larger doses, would cause the same (like) symptoms. Unlike Herbalism, it makes use of natural plants, animals and minerals.

Hypnotherapy prescribes to the thought that it sometimes is necessary to bypass the conscious mind, and enter the unconscious, where repressed emotions, repressed memories and lost experiences (events), are recorded. Some believe that the unconscious mind can receive suggestive thoughts to change behavior, attitudes, and/or emotions which the conscious mind would reject or have difficulty in facilitating.

Laugh Therapy does sound pretty funny (yes I shall keep my day job), but laughing actually does boost your immune system, reduce stress, lower your blood pressure and increases the use of many muscles.

Of all days, the day on which one has not laughed is the one most surely wasted.
- Nicolas Chamfort

Massage Therapy is a very broad term used to describe multiple styles of physical manipulation of muscles, tendons, ligaments of the topical skin and connective tissues (soft body tissue).

Pet Assisted Therapy is the utilization of trained animals to improve the mental and/or physical health of a person. Even though we had pets from the beginning of human kind, it is only recently that pets have been accepted by the mainstream, to be trained to assist in the mental and physical health of individuals. What may come to the mind of most people would be guide dogs for the blind. Although they were instituted primarily for a set of second eyes, studies have found the people who had these guide dogs lived longer, did not have as many ailments, and other such positive side-effects of dog ownership. There are trained therapy animals, which help with all kinds of difficulties, some being the detection of an anxiety attack, early detection of a seizure, as visitors in children's wards, in a therapist' office to help overcome some of the difficulties which can occur when having children as clients, and other such methods.

A therapist can utilize just one of the above listed types of therapy or a mixture of two or more compatible ones to target the whole of a person. If you have researched a therapy which you believe could be a helpful addition to the one you already have chosen, discuss this with your therapist and you might open their eyes to a new method. Many of the therapies do not require a licensed therapist to be the facilitator of; however, it is advantageous for survivors of MST to seek out a therapy or combination of therapeutic techniques, which does include a licensed counselor, in the beginning, to provide amble professional help.

Once again the above listed therapies are not even close to a comprehensive list or description of them; no endorsement is made in the inclusion or exclusion for them into this book. Warning: you can certainly find quacks in conventional therapies as well as alternative therapies, so make inquires, investigate and explore any modality you are thinking about. Any form of therapy which actually improves a client's functionability, decreases the suffering, and does not further wound, is worthy to consider. Just as with the diagnosis, knowledge is power, and I cannot advocate enough to investigate all possible avenues before selecting one.

8
VETERANS ADMINISTRATION

Many women veterans believe they are not "veterans" if they have not served in a combat zone. This is completely untrue. You are a veteran!

Yea, though I walk through the valley of the shadow of death, I will fear no evil: for thou art with me; thy rod and thy staff they comfort me. – Psalms 23:4

Eligibility of using VA

"If you served in the active military service and were separated under any condition other than dishonorable, you may qualify for VA health care benefits. Current and former members of the Reserves or National Guard who were called to active duty by a federal order and completed the full period for which they were called or ordered to active duty may be eligible for VA health benefits as well.

"Most Veterans who enlisted after September 7, 1980, or entered active duty after October 16, 1981, must have served 24 continuous months or the full period for which they were called to active duty in order to be eligible. This minimum duty requirement may not apply to Veterans who were discharged for a disability incurred or aggravated in the line of duty, for a hardship or "early out," or those who served prior to September 7, 1980. Since there are a number of other exceptions to the minimum duty requirements,

VA encourages all Veterans to apply so that we may determine their enrollment eligibility.

"Certain Veterans may be afforded enhanced eligibility status when applying and enrolling in the VA health care system" (va.gov, 2016).

Military Sexual Trauma is determined by the statement of the veteran declaring they experienced MST. Eligibility for services is determined by the VA clinician who decides which problems are related to the MST, other than therapy. Although receiving counseling and/or medical care for problems associated with MST can be thought as admirable from the VA. If you are not granted service-connected status, a medical clinician will establish what is and is not connect to the MST. Filing a claim for Posttraumatic Stress Disorder, Major Depression and/or Anxiety (symptomology from typical Military Sexual Trauma experience) because of symptoms which interfere with your life is not a "hand out." The compensation is not a gift, it is what you deserve. Many MST survivors struggle over being labeled as disabled or having a mental disorder, thereby not receiving their rightful benefits. When you joined the military, you signed a contract which bound you and the government. You held up your side, it is now time for the government to hold up theirs.

Okay, here's the part I get to vent and tell you the horror stories from the VA. Just the ones that happened to me would fill an entire book, so I will only write a few. I have met some of the most professional and honorable people, toward veterans issues, working at the VA. I have also met: people who just want a pay check; power abusing individuals; criminals; liars; perverts; sex offenders; rapists and murderers. Unfortunately, the VA seems to have more of the negatives than the respectable people. At one point, my social worker felt I should go to the VA hospital to get my medications all in order. Through miscommunication, on the VA's part, I was put in a lock-down mental ward, with two see-through gowns on (had to ask for the second, with blood stains on one) until I lied my way out of there. Had I not been able to, I believe I would either be dead or still in the mental institution, locked away, and drugged to zombifyness.

A VA hospital lost me from surgery to my room. My husband and children were told "she didn't make it there" when asked why the surgery was taking so long. You do not say in front of children, that their mom, "didn't make it…" that's all they hear. My husband had to demand they find me, as if just asking where I was and getting the "we don't know," response, was enough. I do understand hospitals are large, but to lose me? It's not like there are so many women veterans in the hospital that I was just in among others. Someone had put me to the side, waiting for a room to get ready (because again, forgetfulness of the VA that I'm a woman and should not be in a hospital room with another guy). Somehow the room was ready but nobody went to find me to put me in it. I can imagine one of those scenes from the movies where the poor unconscious patient is shuffled around the hospital.

I had to use a civilian ER to help with the symptoms from medications I was coming off because the VA doctor's answer was to start taking them again and everything would be better. I've had prostate exams appointments, which I sat in the waiting room for over an hour at one, until someone figured out it probably was a mute appointment. This was when VA just gave appointments, nothing about what it was for, until you got there. I've had the VA not refill my medications because somebody forgot to click a button on their side and I ran out and ended up at the ER (civilian). I've been told that my military experience couldn't happen the way I explained it, because there are rules in the military, this was by a social worker. I've been asked, over the phone, by a male nurse, after I requested to speak with the MST coordinator, "What happened to you?" I've had the front clerks, and much of the staff have no clue what MST stood for. When I said it out, they had no idea there was such a coordinator. When she finally was found, she'd had no idea she'd been assigned that position – for months.

My medications have been mixed up, not refilled, sent to the wrong address, forgot to be inputted by the doctor, pharmacy thought I'd already picked them up (almost called me a liar) and more. I told a nurse I wanted to speak to the doctor before she gave me a shot, she ignored me and stabbed me. After surgery, some nurse tried to yell at me for not telling the doctor about the VA medications I was on – you know that list they have access to, like I was trying to hide something.

I've been told one thing and what was written up in my medical records was completely different. Looked at like there was no way my symptoms were real. Then in the second year I used the VA…just joking (only on the year part). It defiantly is a government run medical institution. I have also gotten some help along the way. I learned early on you must be proactive, direct and sometimes very very stubborn. I ask lots of questions and don't accept excuses. I want to know precisely where in the policy it is; who I can also speak to; how I can get what I need; who is there supervisor; what complaint form do I fill out; and more. I am in charge of my health, and I can be patient, persistent and really really annoying. I try and keep records of everything. I attend C&Ps with my husband, and have him in the room. I take in notes to remember what was essential to talk about. I take notes while in the appointments. I check on doctors, medications, appointments and try to stay updated on changes that effect me. I double check when I'm told something, read the actual policy, procedures, and qualifications. I know how to say no – and I do it. I am purposely vague, as much as their written rules are. I can be just as mind-boggling. I know it's a system set up as an adversary to the health and welfare of all veterans. So, I find the loop-holes, vague wording, double meanings, and use every bit of it to my advantage. That is how you deal with the VA system as a whole.

Referral to the local Readjustment Counseling Service (Vet Center) may also be an appropriate option. Some Vet Centers have specially trained sexual trauma counselors. A list of local VA facilities and Vet Centers can be accessed online at www.va.gov. Also, you can call the VA's general information line 1-800-827-1000.

Military sexual trauma counseling may include individual or group counseling, referral for benefits assistance, liaison with community agencies or substance abuse information and referral to help you deal with the emotions of military sexual trauma and regain confidence in your everyday life. Any veteran who was sexually traumatized while serving in the military is eligible to receive counseling regardless of gender or era of service (va.gov, 2016). But trust your instincts.

VA Disabilities Claims
Filing a Claim
Note: This information is to assist you along with the help of another person to develop your claim. It is not intended and should not be used as the only resource to file your disability claim. Policies change all the time, therefore, this information was the best of my ability at the time it was retrieved.

Before filing a claim, recognize that this most likely will not be a painless, frustrationless journey. The VA claims process is as quick as a snail, assembled with errors and requires constant vigilance to muddle through. It is an adversary to all veterans, and really not intended to be very helpful. Many MST survivors get unnecessarily triggered continuously during the process, but it is not a reason to quit. This will be a very brief chapter about a very extensive subject.

Whether or not you have decided to file a claim for compensation and/or pension at this time, you should obtain a copy of all your military records. There are two types of records: 1) Individual Health and Service Records and 2) Clinical Records. Clinical records are inpatient records filed by the military hospital or other medical facility which provided treatment to you. A summary of your treatment can be listed in your Service Medical Records (SMRs) but does not usually include all the hospital notes and tests.

You can file the claim yourself, which is very unadvisable. You can file with the help of another, and/or seek the help from an accredited Veterans Service Officer (VSO), who typically works for a Veterans Service Organization. It is greatly recommended to have a VSO since there can possibly be a time where the VA sends off a letter stating they have not received evidence. They could say that the time limit is expired, causing you to start from the beginning, or some other process-slowing event. Having an accredited VSO is a backup for these kinds of problems, since all accredited VSOs should document what they have sent and what has been received by the VA, on your behalf. A VSO is not a replacement to finding another veteran to help you through this process. Using someone who has been down this path before is advisable.

To win your claim, three elements are required: a diagnosis, nexus, and evidence.
A diagnosis of the disorder or disease.
For a claim, it is best to have a diagnosis of the disorder or disease, prior to the C&P, but sometimes it doesn't happen like that.

The most effective would come from a competent medical authority on mental health issues; typically a psychiatrist or psychologist, who is either employed by the VA or contracted with them to provide that service. A diagnosis from an outside psychologist/psychiatrist, your VA health care provider or another therapist will also work. However, depending on the licensure they hold or do not hold, it can be considered a recommended diagnosis. You can also be diagnosed at the C&P exam.

MST is not a diagnosis; the diagnosis must come from the DSM-V.

Nexus, link to service

The claimed diagnoses must be linked to a verifiable (stressor) incident. The incident must have been during your service. You will need a letter confirming the nexus (link) of your symptoms to the diagnosis, from a competent medical/mental health authority. If not in your VA medical file, the letter should include a statement, such as: after reviewing (your name)'s medical records it is my opinion, more likely than not, her (diagnosis), is a direct result of military sexual trauma she experienced while serving on active duty. Or during your C&P exam, the examiner agrees the diagnosis is linked to your service and states it within the report.

Evidence

You should first request copies of all your military records (medical plus personnel files), any civilian records from the time you entered and any VA records. There are two types of evidence, what is referred to as direct/primary evidence and then alternative evidence, called - markers. Direct evidence would be formal official documents such as: police reports, rape kit paperwork, crime report, the perpetrator's conviction, and/or the investigator's files.

Many MST survivors never reported the assault/incident(s), or no recorded report was made. Do not be discouraged, there are many avenues for finding alternate evidence or markers. A marker is evidence of behaviors which can occur after having experienced MST. Such behaviors can be: an extreme increase or decrease in performance evaluations; substance abuse; frequent visits to medical facilities with or without diagnosed problems; increase disrespect for military authority (Write-ups, Letter of Reprimands, Article 15, even AWOL); problems with civilian authorities (vandalism, intoxicated in public, and/or shop lifting); marital problems; relationship problems; frequent requests for leave; requests for change of duties, shifts, units, stations; and more. What you are trying to show is that your behavior changed after a certain time. This time being when the incident(s) occurred.

And he said unto me, My grace is sufficient for thee: for my strength is made perfect in weakness. Most gladly therefore will I rather glory in my infirmities, that the power of Christ may rest upon me. - 2 Corinthians 12:9

Your C&P Appointment

Typically you will receive a C&P exam appointment. The time and/or date of the exam may be inconvenient but try to keep this appointment, if at all possible. If you know there is a conflict then as soon as you are aware of the appointment call and change it. Be on time or early for the appointment. If you show up late, depending on how late you are, it can be considered a "no show" and it can take a long time for you to get another appointment.

Understand the C&P exam is going to be terrible. You are going to be asked questions which the answers you may have never discussed with anyone. These questions, to the VA, are necessary to determine your claim and the degree of disability you are suffering from. The questions are not purposely designed to trigger you, the examiner is not trying to be malicious, but these things do happen. It is not recommended that you go to this appointment alone. You will already be distressed, so getting into the driver's seat after or before the appointment, is wrong and hazardous. You should have someone who has been supportive go with you, and even go in to the exam (this depends on your approval only, not another's. If you do not want them in the exam then they should stay out). It can be extremely helpful for your husband to accompany you; lend support, be another source of memories and a witness to the behaviors you have been exhibiting.

Try to keep yourself grounded and in the present during the exam. While you are sitting in the waiting room do not allow yourself to obsess over what the exam will be like and/or what the questions will be. Read a bunch of comic strips you have collected or a funny book or watch videos (with headphones on so that no one else can hear) that can occupy your mind and help you laugh inside. You can use breathing techniques, quick memory joggers, imagery, note taking, doodling or even have a Battle Buddy with you. A Battle Buddy is my own design, a small pocket animal carrying a rucksack with a pleasant aroma. It's designed to calm you and encompasses three of your senses: touch; sight; and especially smell (if you like adding a crinkle in the pack, it engages hearing also). I have tried the worry stone. Sure there was a positive word carved into it, and even though when I rubbed it, it did get hot, in the end it was just a rock. So I thought about the times that I was at my lowest, what helped me through it, and it dawned on me, Killer had. I held him, rubbed his fur, and that soft fur, his eyes, with my prayers brought a smile to my face, at the darkest of times. I researched what would engage most of my senses, and that is what I came up with. It is a type of therapy for me to make them, and I know they head off to help others. Yes, it is a little "stuffed animal" (small to fit in the pocket), but my "fluffy puppy" (what I called Killer) would rip you apart before allowing any harm to come to me. That is what I feel as I hold mine, that feeling of unconditional love and protection.

"VA relaxed its evidentiary standard for disability claims related to MST in 2002 to ensure all available evidence supporting these claims is considered. Because military service records may lack corroborating evidence that a stressful event occurred, VA regulations make clear that evidence from non-military sources may be used to corroborate the Veteran's account of the MST. Further, when direct evidence of an MST is not available, VA may request a medical opinion to consider a Veteran's account and any "markers" to corroborate the occurrence of the MST event as related to current PTSD symptoms.

"Increased awareness of MST issues resulted in special training beginning in December 2011 for all VA regional office personnel who process MST-related claims and the mental health clinicians conducting the examinations related to these claims. This ongoing training focuses on discovering "marker" evidence to support the claim. VA wants all Veterans who filed MST-related PTSD claims before December 2011 to receive the benefits of this nationwide training. If your claim was submitted before that date and denied, you can request a re-evaluation from your local VA regional office.

"Veterans who want VA to review their previously denied MST-related PTSD claim can start by contacting their regional office, calling 1-800-827-1000 or logging into their free eBenefits account at www.eBenefits.va.gov.

"VBA will accept new evidence to be reviewed when a claim is re-evaluated. It's best to send any new evidence at the same time as you request a re-evaluation. Veterans Service Organizations, as well as MST specialists and/or Women Veterans Coordinators available at every VA regional office, can help you determine what type of information is best to submit (va.gov 2016).

Try to not have any other appointments for that day or the next. Have your therapist know when it is and have a plan, all set out, if you need it. Know it will be stressful, prearrange everything you can, it will minimize the influence of it. Know that I am praying for you.

RESOURCES

This is not an exhausted list of all the available resources to you. Many states have their own programs designed for veterans, as well as counties and cities. There literally are thousands of pages of resources out there. As of the time this book was published these were the contacts for these organizations. Because of the internet and the ability to change, some may have changed certain aspects of their programs or their information.

Just Crafty
www.JustCrafty.com

National Center for PTSD
1-802-296-6300 (PTSD Information Center)
www.ptsd.va.gov
www.ncptsd.va.gov

National Institute of Mental Health
www.nimh.nih.gov

National Suicide toll-free hot-line number:
1-800-273-TALK (8255)
www.veteranscrisisline.net

A Black Rose
www.ablackrose.org

AfterDeployment
http://afterdeployment.org

Air Force SAPR
www.afpc.af.mil/library/sapr/index.asp

Air Force Suicide Prevention Program
http://afspp.afm.mil

American Legion
www.legion.org

American Women Veterans Foundation
www.americanwomenveterans.org

American's Heroes at Work
www.americasheroesatwork.gov

Army OneSource Victim Advocacy Program:
www.myarmyonesource.com/FamilyProgramsandSerivces/FamilyPrograms/FamilyAdvocacyProgram/TipfortheHome/default.aspx

Army Sexual Harassment/Assault Reponses Prevention (SHAPR)
www.sexualassault.army.mil

Caregiver Support Line
1-855-260-3274
www.caregiver.va.gov

**Center for the Study of
Traumatic Stress**
www.centerforthestudyoftrauma
ticstress.org

Center for Women Veterans
www1.va.gov/womenvet

**Coalition of Iraq and
Afghanistan Veterans**
www.coalitionforveterans.org

Coast Guard SAPR
www.uscg.mil/worklife/rape_se
xual_assault.asp

**Coast Guard Suicide
Prevention Program**
1-855- CGSUEPT (247-8778)
www.uscg.mil/worklife/suicide
_prevention.asp

**Department of Veteran
Affairs**
MST Homepage
www.mentalhealth.va.gov/msth
ome.asp

**Disabled American Veterans
(DAV)**
www.dav.org

Disibility.gov
www.disability.gov

DoD Safe Helpline
1-877-995-5247
www.safehelpline.org

**DoD Sexual Assault
Prevention and Response
(SAPR)**
www.sapr.mil

Fatigues to Fabulous
fatiguestofabulous.com

Futures without Violence
www.futureswithoutviolence.org

Grace after Fire
www.graceafterfire.org

**International Critical Incident
Stress Foundation**
1-410-750-9600
www.icisf.org

**International Society for
Traumatic Stress Studies**
www.istss.org

**Marine Corps Community
Services**
www.usmc-mccs.org/sapro

Marine Suicide Prevention
www.usmc-
mccs.org/suicideprevent

MedlinePlus Depression
www.nlm.nig.gov/medlineplus/
depression.html

Military Homefront
www.militaryhomefront.dod.mil

Military OneSource:
1-800-342-9647
www.militaryonesource.mil

Military Rape Crisis Center
www.stopmilitaryrape.org

Military Women in Need
www.militarywomeninneed.org

My Healthevet – VA's Personal Health Record:
www.myhealth.va.gov

National Alliance on Mental Illness
1-800-950-NAMI (6264)
www.nami.org

National Center for Post-Traumatic Stress Disorder (PTSD)
1-800-273-8255

National Guard SAPR
www.ng.mil/jointstaff/j1/sapr

National Women's Health Information Center
www.4woman.gov

Navy SAPR
www.cnic.navy.mil

Navy Suicide Prevention
www.suicide.navy.mil

OEF/OIF
www.oefoif.va.gov

OEF/OIF National Guard/Reserves
www.oefoif.va.gov/NationalGuardReserve.asp

One Savvy Veteran
onesavvyveteran.wix.com/womenwarriors

Operation Reinvent
operationreinvent.org

Our Military
www.ourmilitary.mil

Prevention Reporting and Service Member Rights
www.myduty.mil

RAINN (Rape, Abuse & Incest National Network
Hotline: 1-800-656-HOPE (4673)
www.rainn.org

Real Warriors Campaign
www.realwarriors.net

Safe Helpline
www.safehelpline.org

Service Women's Action Network
servicewomen.org

She S.E.R.V.E.D. Inc.
www.she-served.org/

Soldiers' Angels
www.soldiersangels.org

Substance Abuse and Mental Health Services
www.samhsa.gov

The Center for Women Veterans
www.va.gov/WOMENVET

The National Center for Victims of Crime
www.ncvc.org

TRICARE Mental Health Behavior
www.tricare.mil/mybenefit/home/MentalHealthAndBehavior

VA & DoD Post-Traumatic Stress Guidelines
www.healthquality.va.gov/Post_Traumatic_Stress_Disorder_PTSD.asp

VA Center for Veteran Enterprise
www.vetbiz.gov

VA Directive on Pain Management
www1.va.gov/painmanagement

VA Health Benefits Call Center
1-877-222-VETS (8397)
www.va.gov/healtheligibility

VA Mental Health
www.mentalhealth.va.gov

VA Vet Centers
www.vetcenter.va.gov

VetSuccess Online
www.vetsuccess.gov

Veteran Recovery
www.veteranrecovery.org

Veterans of Foreign Wars (VFW)
www.vfw.org

Women in the Military Service for America Memorial (WIMSA)
1-800-222-2294
www.womenmemorial.org

Women's Health Issues and Prevention
www.hooah4health.com/prevention/whealth

Women Veterans Rock
www.womenvetsrock.org

References

1.va.gov/womenvet/page.

American Psychiatric Association: *Diagnostic and Statistical Manual of Mental Disorders*, Fifth Edition, Arlington, VA, American Psychiatric Association, 2013.

And I will make thee whole: helping families with mental health concerns. 2005 Mental Health Resource Foundation, Cedar Fort, Inc.

Barrett, D.H., Doebbeling, C.C., Schwartz, D.A., et al. (2002). Posttraumatic stress disorder and self-reported physical health status among U.S. military personnel serving during the gulf war period. *Psychosomatics, 43 (3),* 195-205.

Butterfield, M., McIntyre, L., Stechuchak, K., Nanda, K., & Bastian, L. (1998). Mental disorder symptoms in veteran women: Impact of physical and sexual assault. *Journal of the American Medical Women's Association, 53,* 198-200.

Campbell, R., & Raja, S. (2005). The sexual assault and secondary victimization of female veterans: Help-seeking experiences with military and civilian social systems. *Psychology of Women Quarterly, 29,* 97-106.

Clum, G.A., Calhoun, K., & Kimmerling, R. (2000). Associations among symptoms of depression and posttraumatic stress disorder and self-reported health in sexually assaulted women. *The Journal of Nervous and mental Disease, 188 (10),* 671-678.

Davis, T., & Wood, P. (1999). Substance abuse and sexual trauma in female veteran population. *Journal of Substance Abuse Treatment, 16 (2),* 123-127.

Defense Centers of Excellence for Psychological Health and Traumatic Brain Injury (DCOE) October 23, 2014 – webinar – *Psychological Health Issues Affecting Women Service Members & Veterans.*

Department of Veterans Affairs. (2004). *Military sexual trauma* (Independent Study Course).

Department of Veterans Affairs. (2009). *The center for women veterans: Counseling & medical treatment for the after affects of sexual trauma.* www.va.gov.

Department of Veterans Affairs. *National Center for PTSD. PTSD treatment programs in the U.S. department of Veterans Affairs.* ptsd.va.gov/public.

Dictionary.references.com/browse/risk (Feb 2016)

Hyun, J.K., Pavao, J., & Kimerling, R. (2009) Military sexual trauma. *PTSD Research Quarterly: Advancing Science and Promoting Understanding of Traumatic Stress, 20* (2).

Karp, S.A., Silber, D.E., Holmstrom, R.W., & Stock, L.J. (1995). Personality of rape survivors as a group and by relation of survivor to perpetrator. *Journal of Clinical Psychology, 51*, 587.

Kasper, P., & White, R. *Help with your VA claims.* mrfa.org/VA.Claim.htm. Retrieved Oct, 2010.

Murdoch, M., & Nichol, K.L. (1995). Women veterans' experiences with domestic violence and with sexual harassment while in the military. *Archives of Family Medicine, 4*, 411-418.

Panagla, S., Bagalman, E., 92014). *Health Care for Veterans: Answers to Frequently Asked Questions.* Congressional Research Service, (7-5700). crs.gov R42747. Retrieved Apr, 2015.

Sadler, A.G., Booth, B.M., Cook, B.L., & Doebbeling, B.N. (2003). Factors associated with women's risk of rape in the military environment. *American Journal of Industrial Medicine, 43*, 262-273.

Sadler, A.G., Booth, B.M., Cook, B.L., Torner, J.C., & Doebbeling, B.N. (2001). The military environment: Risk factors for women's non-fatal assaults. *Journal of Occupational and Environmental Medicine, 43 (4)*, 325-334.

Sadler, A.G., Booth, B., Nielson, D., & Doebbeling, B. (2000). Health-related consequences of physical and sexual violence: Women in the military. *Obstetrics & Gynecology, 96*, 473-480.

Valente, S., & Wight, C. (2007). Military sexual trauma: Violence and sexual abuse. *Military Medicine, 172 (3),* 259-265.

Veterans Health Administraion. *Military sexual trauma (MST) programming:* 1.va.gov/vhapublications.

Vogt, D., Monson, C., Resick, P., & Welch, L. *PTSD 101: Sexual assault and PTSD:* ncptsd.va.gov/ptsd101.

Walker, M. (2007). *Crossing the blue code.* Nebraska: iuniverse.

Walker, M. (2008). *Beyond the blue code.* Nebraska: iuniverse.

Wells, Miette. (2009). *MST: Military Sexual Trauma.* Texas, Wells2000llc.

Wells, Miette. (2011). *MST: Military Sexual Trauma Revised.* Texas, Wells2000llc.

Wells, Miette. (2013). *Understanding Military Sexual Trauma: a guide for those who work with MST survivors.* Texas, Wells2000llc.

Wells, Miette. (2015). *Military Sexual Trauma: a brief overview.* Texas, Wells2000llc.

www.va.gov/healthbenefits/apply/veterans.asp

Zinzow, H., Grubaugh, A., Monnier, J., Suffoletta-Malerie, S., & Freuh, B. (2007). Trauma among female veterans: A critical review. *Trauma, Violence, & Abuse, 8,* 384-400.

Made in the USA
Lexington, KY
19 February 2018